Helping Teens Learn Self-Regulation

Lessons, Activities & Worksheets for Teaching the Essentials of Responsible Decision-Making & Self-Control

A RESOURCE FOR WORKING WITH INDIVIDUALS, SMALL GROUPS AND CLASSROOMS (GRADES 7-12)

by
Brad Chapin, M.S., LCP, LMLP

CD INCLUDED

© 2018, 2016, 2014 YouthLight, Inc.
Chapin, SC 29036

All rights reserved.
Permission is given for individuals to reproduce the activities and worksheet sections in this book.
Reproduction of any other material is strictly prohibited.

Cover and Text Design by Diane Florence
Layout by Melody Taylor
Project Editing by Susan Bowman

ISBN: 978-159850-149-0

Library of Congress Number: 2013955973

10 9 8 7 6 5 4 3
Printed in the United States

Dedication

The author would like to dedicate this book to all of the children, teens and adults who are struggling through life without ever being taught the skills they need to regulate themselves. This book was written in an effort to reach those individuals and provide a sense of hope that things can be better.

Acknowledgements

I would like to thank my family for their support through this continued effort to educate others about the Self-Regulation Training System. I would also like to thank Brooke Stover and her staff for their dedication to helping others learn self-regulation skills in order to be happier, healthier and more successful.

Table of Contents

Section 1: Introduction
Diagram of Framework 7
Assumptions 8
Research 9

Section 2: Introductory Lessons: Self-Regulation Equals Success
Keys to My Success 18
My Path to Success 21
Regulate for Success 24

Section 3: Physical Strategies
The Warning System 27
Alarms and False Alarms 30
Short Fuse 32
My Warning Signs 35
Create a Safe Place 38
Mobile Safety 41
Stretching and Movement 43
Taking Advantage of the Senses 46
Routines and Predictability 49
Physical Regulation Review for Mastery 52

Section 4: Emotional Strategies
What's Your Status 56
Feelings Playlist 58
Sticky Feelings 61
Emotional Build-up 62
Advice Blog 65
Top 10 List 68
Healthy Expression Skits 70

Table of Contents

Expression Style Quiz 72
You Can't Make Me Smile 75
Who's in Control 78
Declaration of Emotional Freedom 81
Mind Control 82
Emotional Knots 86
Emotional Regulation Review for Mastery 88

Section 5: Cognitive Strategies

Healthy Emotional Boundaries with Technology – "WWSWW Zones" 92
Extreme Thinking 95
Calculated Risk-taking 98
Evidence Piles 101
More Dirty Words 104
Getting What You Really Want – Freedom 106
Control Debate 109
Juggling Life 111
Cognitive Regulation Review for Mastery 114

Section 6: Putting it All Together

Share What You've Learned with Project-based Learning 118
Plan of Action 120
Celebrate Success 124

Section 7: Core Curriculum Guide

12-Session Core Curriculum for Self-Regulation Training 127
Appendices A–H: 130
References 140
About the Author 141

Section 1: Introduction

Why Focus on Self-Regulation?

As a professional in these fast-paced times, we are constantly faced with the challenges of demonstrating outcomes, operating on a tight budget, working long hours, and serving a population that often seems more intense and challenging every day. With all of these pressures, it is easy to become overwhelmed. As a parent raising children in these times, we are faced with a number of new challenges and pressures. Helping our children learn the skills they need to succeed has never been more difficult.

Even when simply trying to figure out how we can help, the challenge of sifting through numerous research articles, books, and approaches developed during the past several decades can feel overwhelming. A primary goal of the Self-Regulation Training System is to keep things practical, simple and effective. Over the years, I have filtered through thousands of pieces of information to find common themes and patterns that are effective. The driving force behind this strategy guide is this question.

"If you had only 5 or 10 minutes to spend helping an individual, what is the most important set of skills you could teach?"

With so many teens struggling in so many areas, how could there be one answer to this question? After working with hundreds of families, reading countless books and articles, conducting research, and speaking with parents and professionals around the country, the answer has become clear. I found myself returning to the same core strategies. They are practical and they work! It can be summed up with one term . . . Self-Regulation.

Sadly, as I've traveled around the country speaking on this topic, I've found that very few people really have a good understanding of Self-Regulation. Yet, there is an intense hunger for a practical approach to teach teens concrete skills that will help them achieve success in all areas of their lives. This simple framework can demystify complex issues and provide clear direction for skill-training.

The term Self-Regulation is no longer reserved for impulse-control issues. Self-Regulation is a broad term that encompasses most of the major issues we see people struggling with. In the literature, Self-Regulation, or this concept of regulating one's physical, emotional and behavioral responses, has been closely associated with several other terms including emotional regulation, self-control, and coping (Macklem, 2008). In the spirit of presenting simple, practical and useful information, the philosophy and strategies contained in this book are based on a broad and flexible definition of Self-Regulation.

Section 1: Introduction

Based on my interpretation of the literature and experience in the field, I have come to understand that Self-Regulation is a universal set of skills directly related to success in every major area of functioning. In fact, Shonkoff & Phillips (2000) refer to Self-Regulation as a cornerstone of childhood development that cuts across all domains of behavior. It predicts academic success better than IQ (Duckworth & Seligman, 2005). It also correlates highly with longevity and well-being (Grossarth-Maticek & Eysenck, 1995; Moffitt et al., 2011). In other words, those who regulate themselves well have higher academic performance, are more successful and live longer, happier lives than those who do not.

This list is not complete, but it should help you determine whether or not this book is for you. If you are a parent or your profession involves helping children, teens or adults with any of these topics, you will find this information to be useful, practical and effective.

This is a short list of additional topics related to Self-Regulation:

Academic Performance	Cognitive Flexibility	Locus of Control	Self-efficacy
Aggression/Violence	Depression	Happiness	Self-esteem
Anger	Emotional Control	Oppositional Defiance	Social interaction
Anxiety	Executive Function	Mood Regulation	Success
Attention	Impulse Control	Motivation	Trauma
Attribution	Learned Helplessness	School Safety	

What Are the Strategies Based on?

In an effort to save time, I will use a simple diagram of the philosophy and condense a great deal of the information supporting this program down into eight assumptions. Approaching serious issues without a framework or philosophy to operate from can be devastating. You can feel confused and overwhelmed. Your attempts to help will not only seem scattered and confusing to you, but also to the individual you are working with. The chances of success will diminish significantly. This diagram illustrates the fundamental framework for the approach.

Section 1: Introduction

Diagram of Self-Regulation Training Philosophy

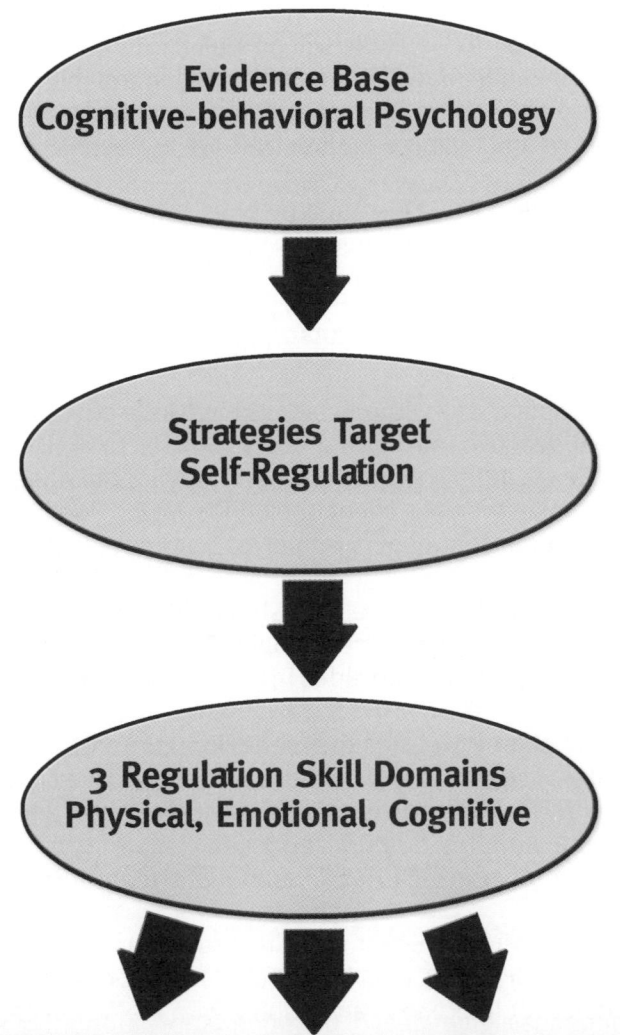

Academic Performance	Emotional Control	Motivation
Aggression/Violence	Executive Function	School Safety
Anger	Impulse Control	Self-efficacy
Anxiety	Learned Helplessness	Self-esteem
Attention	Locus of Control	Social interaction
Attribution	Longevity	Success
Cognitive Flexibility	Happiness	Trauma
Depression	Oppositional Defiance	Well-being

Section 1: Introduction

The following list of eight Assumptions provides the supporting principles for the framework. Many of these assumptions are consistent with Cognitive-Behavioral psychology.

Assumption #1 – People will do well if they can. It is our job as responsible adults to help others navigate and remove barriers in their lives (Greene & Ablon, 2006). We do not believe that we are here to control others. Our goal is for children/teens to grow and manage themselves. We are helpful guides in the process.

Assumption #2 – One must be physically calm and feel safe to effectively engage in problem-solving, perform well and learn (Yerkes & Dodson, 1908; Goleman, 1998). We know from medical, educational, and psychological studies that higher level brain functions are impaired during times of physical distress. This applies to both children, teens and adults.

Assumption #3 – Human beings have little control over their environment, but a great deal of control over their responses to their environment. Our perception of the event is more powerful, with regards to our emotional and behavioral response, than the event itself (Ellis, 1962). We must first believe that we can have some control over ourselves before we will attempt to change (Kuhl, 1984).

Assumption #4 – The relationship is likely the most important variable when trying to help someone change (Hubble, Duncan & Miller, 1999). This assumption has been replicated for decades in the psychological research literature.

Assumption #5 – Cognitive-behavioral psychology works. Strategies from the realm of cognitive-behavioral psychology have consistently been shown to effectively help individuals change their mood and behavior. There are now several hundred randomized research studies to support this approach (Beck & Fernandez, 1998; Butler, Chapman, Forman & Beck, 2006).

Assumption #6 – Effective Self-Regulation is critical for success and happiness. Those individuals who have well-developed Self-Regulation skills have a better chance for happiness and coping with life's challenges (Baumeister, Heatherton, & Tice, 1994; Duckworth & Seligman, 2005; Masten & Coatsworth, 1998).

Assumption #7 – In order to be effective, we need to meet people where they are currently functioning (Greene & Ablon, 2006; Bailey, 2001). Not matching your strategies to fit the individual's current level of skill will result in frustration and failure.

Assumption #8 – Do not assume that the individual has learned anything about how to regulate their own behaviors in a healthy way. Many people we work with have not had exposure to positive self-regulatory examples. With the right strategies and information, people can change their thoughts and behaviors.

Section 1: Introduction

If we don't believe people are capable of change, we are all wasting a great deal of time and energy.

To be consistent with the practical efforts of this framework, much of the information supporting this approach has been condensed into the assumptions. If you have questions about these assumptions, please feel free to research the information further, or contact the author of this book.

One important barrier we all face when working with individuals is the challenge of engagement. The individual must be engaged in the process for it to be successful. A great deal of experience with this idea was gained during the creation and implementation of the Challenge Software Program for children. This unique, web-based tool utilizes animated scenarios and games to engage children quickly and teach them the basics of self-control. It can be found at www.cpschallenge.com. In line with the theme of the Challenge Software Program and the previous book, "Helping Young People Learn Self-Regulation" for K-6 children, the strategies in this book are designed to be engaging and fun.

What About Research, Assessment, and Outcomes?

We have compiled data on several hundred students at different grade levels who have completed 12 sessions of Self-Regulation Training. These 20-30 minute lessons were taught by teachers and mental health professionals. The results have been outstanding. In one study of 380 first-graders, the average score on the Self-Regulation Teacher Rating Scale (see Appendix) improved from a score of 72 to 87, which is extremely statistically significant. In another study, office discipline referrals were reduced by 83% over a three-month period following the 12 sessions. Significant results were also demonstrated by the Self-Regulation Self-Report Questionnaire (see appendix). Research on more longitudinal factors is ongoing.

Major changes were also documented in how classroom teachers conceptualized behavioral issues and responded to problems. After teaching the 12 sessions, teachers consistently reported increased insight into how their own Self-Regulation skills impact situations. They also reported feeling more confident in understanding behaviors as well as a new-found competence in knowing exactly how to help a struggling student with an effective intervention based on a solid framework. Additionally, teachers reported feeling like they had more time for instruction because the students had learned the skills necessary for managing behaviors on their own.

Section 1: Introduction

What Are the 3 Areas of Self-Regulation Training?

When regulating one's self, one must have skills for calming the body, skills for expressing emotions appropriately, and skills for moderating thoughts to problem-solve effectively. Therefore, it makes sense to divide Self-Regulation into 3 Functional Categories (Chapin & Penner, 2012).

> **3 Functional Categories of Self-Regulation**
> 1. Physical
> 2. Emotional
> 3. Cognitive

The following few paragraphs offer a short description of the relevance for these 3 functional domains.

Physical Regulation

> **Focus on:**
> - Recognizing Warning Signs
> - Getting Safe & Calm

First, we must revisit Assumption #2. This assumption indicates that we cannot engage in any of our other interventions until the individual is calm. Therefore, teaching the physical strategies that focus on calming should be a priority and come first.

At the most basic level, the physical component of Self-Regulation consists of moderating the fight/flight stress response in the lower regions of the brain, or Brain Stem. When the stress response in the brain stem is activated, chemical reactions take place in the body that cause adrenaline and cortisol to be released. Additionally, the heart rate and blood-flow to the major muscle groups increase in an effort to prepare the body to fight or run (Cannon, 1932). The capacity for activity in the higher portions of the brain, required for effective problem-solving, is decreased. Therefore, it's critical that we learn to deactivate this stress response before we move forward with higher level interventions.

Physical Strategies Include:

- Recognizing Warning Signs
- Repetitive, patterned movement involving the major muscle groups (Ex. – Stretching)
- Regulation of breathing (Ex. – deep breathing exercises)
- Redirection or distraction (Ex. – leaving the stressful situation)
- Bilateral Stimulation of the brain – activities that engage both sides of the brain (Ex. – Crossing and uncrossing your arms or legs)

Section 1: Introduction

The importance of developing physical calming skills for good Self-Regulation cannot be over-stated. In line with Assumption #7, almost all problem-situations involve some degree of Brain Stem activation and the need to implement physical strategies first in order to move forward. As with most skills, development of adequate physical calming skills requires practice when the individual is in a non-stressed state. In Chapter 2, we will provide you with several ideas for addressing physical regulation.

Emotional Regulation
Focus on:
- **Identifying Emotions**
- **Expressing Emotions in Healthy Ways**
- **Owning Responsibility for Our Emotions**

As stated in Assumption #6, effective regulation is crucial for emotional well-being. One of the major goals of improving emotional regulation is teaching the individual about his/her ability to control his/her own emotional responses to events. But before addressing this concept with teens, some basic skills need to be in place. First, the individual needs to have some language to label their emotions accurately. When a person is experiencing an intense emotion, one of the first things we want them to do is to communicate that feeling using words. This not only indicates to others what the individual is feeling, but also engages higher functioning areas of the brain and can start the calming process.

Secondly, emotional regulation requires the ability to express emotions in healthy ways. This typically includes the utilization of physical calming skills to moderate the feeling that is being expressed. Emotions can be expressed in many ways. Some ways are healthy, and some ways are unhealthy and can cause damage to the individual and/or others around them. Some people have a tendency to internalize emotions and some have a tendency to externalize emotions. Learning healthy ways to express our emotions significantly impacts our ability to be successful.

The third area of emotional regulation involves learning about how much control we have over our own emotions. Drawing on Assumption #3, this task of convincing individuals to focus on what they can control is crucial for success. If you don't address this issue successfully, your other interventions may not work because the individual will not "believe" he/she can do anything about the issue. This is also a very empowering lesson for a person to learn. He/she will learn that other people and events don't dictate his/her feelings and behaviors. They will also realize that they have been allowing other people and events to "control" them. This shift in thinking is very important in order to move forward and bridges the gap into Cognitive Regulation. Section 4 provides strategies that you can use to help teens become better at identifying, expressing, and controlling their emotions.

Section 1: Introduction

Cognitive Regulation
  Focus on:
  - Identifying and Challenging Unhealthy/Extreme Thinking
  - Planning/Organizational Skills
  - Problem-solving
  - Gaining Insight into Motives and Healthy Ways to Get Psychological Needs Met
  - Self-monitoring/Reinforcement of Healthy Behaviors

Equally as important as the physical and emotional domains of Self-Regulation, is the development of cognitive regulation skills. This higher skill level involves more critical thinking, self-monitoring, and the development of insight. Within this domain we are developing the abilities to modify thoughts, explore motives, plan responses, process events, problem-solve and prevent problems.

Cognitive regulation also allows us to focus on specific problem areas and examine the benefits of personal strengths. This skill-training area is designed to increase insight and promote understanding of patterns that may not be working well and correct them. Chapter 4 addresses many common issues teens struggle with today using lessons related to stress, self-esteem, independence, risk-taking behaviors, anger and relationships.

Why Focus on Self-Regulation in Adolescence?

Adolescence is a time of many challenges and transitions. There are significant physical, emotional, and cognitive changes taking place during this phase of life. How one manages these issues is critical for success. Many of the struggles in adolescence are connected to our desire for independence. During this time-period, we are preparing physically, emotionally, and cognitively to leave home. As part of this transition, we are creating our own unique identity and learning how to manage significant relationships with others.

From what we have covered in this chapter so far, it's likely quite clear how critical Self-Regulation skills are for successfully navigating adolescence and preparing teenagers for success and happiness as an adult. When we leave home, there is no one there to regulate us. We must be able to manage ourselves in order to succeed.

Section 1: Introduction

How do I Use this Book?

In line with the practical philosophy, this approach is designed to be applied in a flexible manner and implemented in many different settings. The strategies can be used individually or with small groups. These skills are universal and necessary for success in most areas of life. This is why many schools are finding that the Self-Regulation Training System is an excellent common core for teaching healthy behavior. The skills and strategies are important for all students and can easily be implemented into the general education population. This approach is also useful for high risk and identified populations, who often struggle significantly with Self-Regulation. Additionally, these strategies lend themselves to being used one-at-a-time for specific issues, or as an organized set of lessons to maximize Self-Regulation and skill development.

The diagram of the supporting philosophy (p.131) illustrates the simple and practical flow of this approach. It is based soundly in cognitive-behavioral psychology and targets the 3 areas of Self-Regulation training: Physical, Emotional, and Cognitive. We recommend that individuals move progressively through the functional domains by first developing the Physical skills, then Emotional skills, and finally the Cognitive skills. As the diagram indicates, there are several problem areas that you can target with this approach.

As with any approach, the first step is a good assessment. When working individually with a child, complete a brief assessment using the individual's background information and the provided Assessment/Progress Monitoring Tool (p.130) to identify strengths and needs regarding physical, emotional and cognitive regulation skills. This will provide you with direction on which type of strategies you will need to focus on the most.

Most individuals will need to start with physical strategy development, then move to emotional skills, and lastly to the cognitive skills. Please remember to consider the developmental and cognitive ability levels when setting goals for skill development. Individuals with cognitive impairments may not be ready for the Cognitive strategies. However, even very young children can learn to master the Physical and Emotional strategies.

The following example illustrates how the Assessment/Progress Monitoring Tool guides the process from the beginning stages of assessment through the implementation of specific strategies and progress monitoring. As you can see from the example, this simple tool provides a concise summary of the issues addressed, the strategies used to target the issues, and the individual's progress toward the development of Self-Regulation skills within each of the skill domains.

Section 1: Introduction

Example:
James is a 14-year-old boy who is often disruptive in class. He has frequent anger outbursts. Once he becomes angry, he stays agitated for over an hour and continues to struggle when he returns to class. These outbursts can be triggered by other students or by the teacher. He seems to believe that "things have to be a certain way or else" and it is obvious that he does not believe he has control over his actions. He believes that others "make" him angry and can be openly defiant. His grades and cognitive abilities are average for his age. He comes from a single-parent home. These behaviors are also being reported at home.

Section 1: Introduction

James – Individual Assessment/Progress Monitoring Tool over an 8-week Period:

	Behaviors To Address/Goals	1st Rating (1-10)	Strategy Used (See Matrix)	Response	Outcome Rating (1-10)
PHYSICAL					
Recognizes physical signs	Explosive outbursts, poor recognition	1	My Warning Signs	Completed first week, continue to practice	8
Uses healthy calming strategies successfully	Stays escalated for extended periods, Needs development	1	Short Fuse, Mobile Safety	Mastered after 3 weeks, Calms down much quicker	7
EMOTIONAL					
Identifies feelings	Only Anger, Needs development	1	What's Your Status	Much better at labeling	8
Recognizes responsibility and ability to change	Blames others for his outbursts	1	Who's in Control	Enjoyed activity, still working at this concept	6
Expresses emotions in healthy ways	Stuffs feelings or is aggressive	2	Emotional Build-up, Feelings Playlist	Developing health outlets	7
COGNITIVE					
Replaces unhealthy thoughts with healthy beliefs	Rigid, black and white thinking	2	Extreme Thoughts, More Dirty Words	Can identify unhealthy thoughts, still working on challenging them	6
Uses cognitive strategies to problem-solve	No healthy plan to get needs met	1	Getting What You Really Want – Freedom	Some insight into better ways to get normal need met	6
STRENGTHS: Likes music, smart, has friends, good at sports			**BARRIERS:** Rigid thinking, anger has built up, difficult to build rapport with		

©YouthLight | 15

Section 1: Introduction

In addition to using the strategies to build your own tailored curriculum based on the individual needs of each teen, the final chapter of this book contains an example of a 12-Lesson Core Curriculum. This core can be used with small groups or entire classrooms and it provides a solid foundation of self-regulation skills to build upon.

Goals and Expectations

The intent of this book is to provide you with practical, effective and engaging strategies that can be easily implemented to address a wide variety of common issues to help individuals succeed. Ideally, teaching and learning Self-Regulation involves more than just working through a set of interventions. It is a philosophy for understanding and addressing the challenges of life. Self-Regulation involves learning and implementing a skill set that is crucial for success and overall well-being.

The flexibility of the Self-Regulation Training System allows you to incorporate many of the techniques you already use. If you were to review your favorite interventions, you would find that many of them will easily fit into this model. They could be categorized within the areas of Physical, Emotional or Cognitive strategies. We encourage you to use this framework to help organize your approach and incorporate your favorite strategies, your interests and your unique specialties to make it your own. The practical layout of this approach allows you to easily create a curriculum that is tailor-made for each individual, or group, that you work with.

It is evident that we will never have the time, energy or resources to specifically train individuals how to respond to each of the thousands of difficult situations they will encounter in a lifetime one-by-one. We will not be able to identify every single trigger (antecedent) that could potentially throw a person off course, or follow them around to be sure we provide the appropriate consequence for each of their behaviors. We will never be able to make life go perfectly, or control how others treat them. It's also very unlikely that we will be able to identify and successfully challenge each of the unhealthy thoughts they may have. Given our limitations, it makes sense that we provide them with the effective "tools" necessary to cope with these situations on their own. Helping people develop self-regulatory skills will provide them with the ability to make healthy choices about their thoughts, feelings and behaviors on their own in most situations. That is our wish for each person and the purpose of this approach.

Section 2
Introductory Lessons: Self-Regulation Equals Success

A major challenge in working with teenagers is engagement. This is the stage of questioning, and adults working with this population are consistently tasked with answering the question, "Why should we do this?" This section of the book provides lessons designed to answer this question.

Self-Regulation skills are highly related to success in many areas. The lessons in this section can provide the motivation to learn these skills and help make the connection between Self-Regulation and success.

Use one or more of these lessons to begin a curriculum, or set of lessons, you plan to administer. This way you will have set the tone for the underlying theme of success and will have answered the question, "Why should we do this?" The focus for strategies in this section is engagement. This also provides the reference point for relating the skills they are about to learn back to success and happiness.

Introductory Lessons: Self-Regulation Equals Success

The Keys to My Success

Purpose Decades of research clearly indicate Self-Regulation skills are critical for success and happiness. The lessons contained in the following sections of this book focus on skills in three categories of Self-Regulation. As you move through the lessons, it's important to reflect on the skills that have been learned. The Keys to My Success tracking sheet can be used to track the progression of skills as you guide individuals through a set of lessons. Complete this worksheet as you move through lesson of Physical, Emotional, and Cognitive Regulation. When complete, this will provide a simple, one-page summary of the individualized skills learned by the participants.

Materials
- The Keys to My Success tracking sheet

Process

1. Begin by reading this short story:

   → "Sara is a freshman. She is an above-average student with dreams of going to college and eventually becoming a writer… or a journalist… or maybe a doctor. She's not quite sure. She also wants to have a family, a nice house, and be happy."

2. Next, pose these questions:

   → "What are some of the challenges Sara may face over the next several years that could get in the way of her reaching her dreams?"

   → "What skills, other than those learned in her school classes, might she need to reach her dreams?"

   → "How will she know what to do? Because what she does will determine her success or failure."

3. Guide the discussion toward the discovery that many of the skills required for reaching our dreams of success and happiness may be outside the general areas of math, reading, and science. Also, be sure to point out that it's important not to get caught-up in discussing events that may happen in Sara's life that she cannot control.

Section 2
Introductory Lessons: Self-Regulation Equals Success

The Keys to My Success (continued)

4. Express that over several decades, researchers have identified "Key" skills that lead to success and happiness in life. Individuals with these skills live longer, happier lives and are more likely to be successful in school, in relationships, and in reaching their goals. Let your participants know that many people do not know about these skills because they were never taught. Indicate that you recognize how valuable these skills are, and how important it is to share these skills with individuals you know.

5. Present the participants with The Keys to My Success tracking sheet. Complete the tracking over the next several weeks as you progress through the lessons.

Note: If you will be using a folder for students to keep all of their subsequent Self-Regulation Training lessons in, you may want to attach The Keys to My Success tracking sheet to the inside cover for easy reference.

Worksheet

The Keys to My Success

Physical Regulation Skills   Check When Learned

    My Warning Signs: _____

_____   _____

    My Safe Place: _____

_____   _____

    My Calming: _____

_____   _____

Emotional Regulation Skills   Check When Learned

    Label Feelings: _____

_____   _____

    Express Feelings in Healthy Ways: _____

_____   _____

    Own My Feelings: _____

_____   _____

Cognitive Regulation Skills   Check When Learned

    Recognize & Challenge Unhealthy Thoughts:

_____

_____   _____

    Motives/Planning/Strengths/Rewards: _____

_____   _____

Introductory Lessons: Self-Regulation Equals Success

My Path to Success

Purpose Connecting the present with the future can be a challenge for tweens and teens. Although, it may be difficult for adolescents to see how their current behaviors can impact their future, we cannot avoid the subject. This lesson is designed to connect the skills they will learn from the Self-Regulation training activities to reaching their future goals.

Materials
- My Path worksheet, writing utensil

Process
1. Begin the discussion with encouraging statements about success and reaching goals. You may state that there are certain strategies proven to help people reach their goals, live longer, be happier and more successful. Also, indicate that there are many things that can get in the way of success.

2. Hand out the worksheet and help students identify those barriers to success. Discuss how these barriers are often out of our control. Discuss issues that are also within our control.

3. Discuss the idea of leaving our success to chance, or taking steps to increase our ability to reach our goals (See Variation).

4. Identify strengths and skills we have that will increase our chances of reaching success. If you are planning on teaching the Physical, Emotional, and Cognitive Self-Regulation skills in a later session, you may want to leave room to enter these skills as they are progressively taught and continue to refer back to this worksheet.

Variation Create, or purchase, a Plinko™ board. Create cards indicating typical ideas of success (money, friends, living longer, being happy, etc.) along with cards indicating failure to place at the bottom of the board. Use only one or two success cards and several cards for indicating failure for each demonstration. Ask the students about leaving their success up to chance versus learning skills to increase their chances. After demonstrating the game with several results of failure, string a ribbon through the pegs of the board to create a path to the success card. Be sure to indicate that the ribbon represents skills we can learn to navigate the barriers (pegs) that happen in our lives. Without the skills, we are simply bouncing around through life and have a greater chance of not reaching our goals.

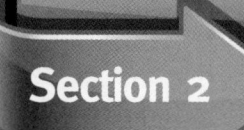

Introductory Lessons: Self-Regulation Equals Success

My Path to Success (continued)

Challenge If you plan to deliver several lessons over a period of time to a classroom or small groups, designate several small group leaders that will send group texts/emails between sessions with reminders. These reminders can include short messages about the lessons or statements to encourage group members to use the skills they've learned. The group leaders may also send out questions, or generate a group dialogue with real life examples of situations where individuals have used Physical, Emotional, or Cognitive Self-Regulation skills.

Discussion Questions

1. What do you think about people spending so much time trying to control things that they can't control? And so little time on the things they can control?

2. How does learning skills to be successful at life relate to learning skills to be successful in other areas like school or sports?

3. How and when do we learn and practice the skills we need to overcome barriers, or challenges in our life? Where do we learn how to handle anger, fear, or sadness?

4. What skills, other than reading, writing, and math, are important for success in life?

Worksheet

My Path to Success

My Goals – What success looks like to me:

1. _____
2. _____
3. _____

Skills I need to reach my goals

1. _____
2. _____
3. _____
4. _____

Strengths I have to help me reach my goals:

1. _____
2. _____
3. _____
4. _____

What could get in the way of my success?

1. _____
2. _____
3. _____
4. _____

Now, place a check next to the items you have the most control over.

©YouthLight

Section 2 — Introductory Lessons: Self-Regulation Equals Success

Regulate For Success

Purpose — In order for any system to be successful, self-monitoring and Self-Regulation strategies need to be in place. This activity is designed to simulate the interaction between a system, its individual parts and its ability to be monitored and regulated to successfully accomplish the goal. This lesson will help to engage individuals in the process and set the stage for progressing into other lessons.

Materials — One ball for each group

Process

1. Begin the discussion with encouraging statements about success and reaching goals. You may state that there are certain strategies proven to help people reach their goals, live longer, be happier and more successful.

2. Ask about success. You may ask, "What does success look like? Who can you name that is successful?"

3. Now, introduce the concept of systems. Ask for examples of systems (solar system, water system, etc.). Indicate that systems are all around us and we are made up of several systems (digestive system, respiratory system, immune system, etc.).

4. Indicate how important it is for systems to learn how to be successful. You may give examples of what happens when different systems stop working, become unbalanced or unregulated.

5. State that this activity will simulate a system with several working parts, or smaller systems, attempting to reach a goal successfully. There will be challenges and forces at work that make success more difficult. The system will need to adjust to increase the chances for success.

6. Give each group a ball. State that the goal is for each person to touch the ball three times without the ball dropping. Group members must toss the ball from person to person. Notice the strategies used by each system to accomplish the task.

7. Once the group(s) have accomplished the first task, introduce the next challenge. State that the goal is the same. Each person must touch the ball three times without the ball dropping, but this time they must go in alphabetical order by each person's first name. Note the strategies used.

8. Next, repeat the game, but this time they must go in alphabetical order by last name. Note the strategies used.

9. Next, repeat the game one last time, but this time they must put one hand behind their back. Note the strategies used.

Introductory Lessons: Self-Regulation Equals Success

Regulate For Success (continued)

10. Process the different strategies used by the group(s). Name all of the variables that were out of their control. Draw attention to the fact that each individual could only control their own piece of the larger system. Emphasize that many variables are out of our control, but our success can be determined by how we adjust to these challenges.

Challenge

If you plan to deliver several lessons over a period of time to a classroom or small groups, designate several small group leaders that will send group texts/emails between sessions with reminders. These reminders can include short messages about the lessons or statements to encourage group members to use the skills they've learned. The group leaders may also send out questions, or generate a group dialogue with real life examples of situations where individuals have used Physical, Emotional, or Cognitive Self-Regulation skills.

Discussion Questions

1. Think about our environment and the possible effects of global warming. What caused the warming? What can the system do to bring it back into balance?

2. Give several examples of how systems can recognize when there is a problem and fix it (ex. thermostat).

3. Explain how the following statement relates to the activity and to success in life. "Each person can only control his/her own thoughts, feelings and actions."

Section 3: Physical Strategies

Physical Strategies

As we mentioned in Section 1, there is a logical reason for starting with the physical regulation skills. In order to be able to discuss emotions and engage in problem-solving we must be physically calm. Individuals who haven't developed this skill are still regularly operating in a fight/flight/shut-down mode that inhibits their ability to progress. When people are in this state, they are not able to learn or benefit from common forms of intervention. They are not open to rational communication or problem-solving and may not respond well to traditional forms of behavior modification.

The importance of having well-developed physical calming skills cannot be overstated. From my experience, even a child with the most serious of issues can function in the home or learning environment if they can physically calm themselves down before they explode. So, before initiating higher level interventions, or expecting individuals to make progress, be sure they have developed the skills necessary for physical regulation.

The following interventions are designed to teach the basic skills of physical regulation. There are three main functional skill-training areas within the Physical Regulation domain:

- Identification of physical warning signs for upset
- Learning how to get safe to deactivate the warning system
- Learn and implement calming skills

The lessons can be used one at a time, or as part of a set curriculum to address a specific problem area. Remember to use the Assessment/Progress Monitoring Tool (p.130) to help you decide which physical strategies to use based on the problem areas you want to address.

Note: The physical strategies are <u>the only</u> strategies that should be implemented when an individual is upset. They should <u>not</u> be taught when a child is upset, but instead, practiced until mastery ahead of time so the individual knows exactly what to do when the stress response is triggered.

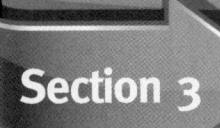

Physical Strategies

The Warning System

Purpose Our bodies are equipped with a built-in warning system that alerts us when a threat is detected. The purpose of this warning system is survival. When this system is activated, it is our clue that we need to do something. It is what we choose to do that dictates the outcome of the situation.

This lesson introduces the concept of our internal warning system in comparison to other warning systems.

Materials
- Warning System Worksheet, writing utensil

Process

1. Introduce the purpose of a warning system and hand out the worksheet. You may say something like:

   → "There are examples of warning systems all around us. These warning systems tell us when something is about to happen. They are there to protect us."

2. Together, generate common examples of warning systems in our environment (example: tornado siren, fire alarm, vehicle dash-board lights) to complete the first section of the worksheet.

3. Discuss each example and how these warning systems relate to survival and safety.

4. Now, connect these examples to our human warning system. You may say something like:

   → "Did you know that we all have our own internal warning system? When our brain detects something that may be threatening to us, it sets off the alarm in our body. When we are hungry, our stomach may growl. When we are tired, we may yawn. But what about when our brain decides that something may be threatening our feelings? Our bodies also have a warning system for this type of threat."

5. Generate a list of the signals our body uses to tell us that something is wrong, or an emotional threat has been detected (example: heart beats faster, eyes widen) and complete this section of the worksheet.

Section 3: Physical Strategies

The Warning System (continued)

Discussion Questions
1. How does the brain know when to activate the alarm system?
2. How is the human alarm system the same, or different, from other alarm systems?
3. When and where do you feel signs that your warning system is activated?

Variations Small Group – Break into teams to see how many examples each team can generate.

Use the Internet to search alarm systems to view diagrams and other examples of warning systems the group did not identify.

Challenge The next time you notice your warning system has engaged, write down the threat. It may also be possible to email or text this information to a central location to generate a list for follow-up discussion.

Worksheet

The Warning System

List 5 examples of Warning Systems (example: tornado siren, dash board of a car):

1. _____
2. _____
3. _____
4. _____
5. _____

List 5 Ways Our Body Tells Us Something Is Wrong:

1. _____
2. _____
3. _____
4. _____
5. _____

Discussion Questions

1. How does the brain know when to activate the alarm system?

   _____

   _____

2. How is the human alarm system the same, or different, from other alarm systems?

   _____

   _____

3. When and where do you feel signs that your warning system is activated?

   _____

   _____

Section 3: Physical Strategies

Alarms and False Alarms

Purpose

Although our warning system is in place to protect us from threats, there are many times when this alarm system over-functions given the situation. The alarm is triggered whenever our brain "perceives" that something may be a threat. This means that if we misperceive something as a threat when it really isn't threatening, our alarm system may still be triggered.

Additionally, it is important to know that our alarm system responds to an emotional threat in the same way it responds to a physical threat. This means that our body may respond the same way to a failure or loss of a friendship as it would if we were being chased by a tiger.

This lesson is designed to help identify when our alarm system may be over-functioning.

Materials

- False Alarms Worksheet, writing utensil

Process

1. Introduce the concept of False Alarms in connection with our physical warning system. You may say something like:

   → "We are all equipped with an internal warning system. The alarm is triggered when we believe something is threatening us. However, there are times that our alarm system is triggered, but we aren't in any real danger. There are also times when there may be a threat, but our body goes into high alert when the threat is small."

2. Discuss the idea of degrees. Our alarm system can be activated, deactivated, and operate at different levels of intensity and duration.

3. Use the scenarios and questions on the worksheet to illustrate this concept. Complete the worksheet individually or as a group.

Discussion Questions

1. What are some examples of when your alarm system may have over-functioned? Have you heard the term "over-react?" What do you think it means and is it related?

2. What are some examples of times when your alarm system may have under-functioned?

3. What are the consequences of your alarm system over-functioning? Under-functioning?

Worksheet

Alarms and False Alarms

Read each scenario and fill in the blanks.

Scenario #1
"Jenny was reading through her friend's social networking page and saw a comment that her friend had posted about liking Jenny's boyfriend."

What might seem threatening to Jenny? _____

What might some of her warning signs be? _____

How intense might her warning signs be and how long might they last? _____

Scenario #2
"Jason was planning on going to hang out with his friends on Friday night. When he asked his Mother if he could go, she reminded him that she had planned for them to go and visit their Grandmother on Friday night."

What might seem threatening to Jason? _____

What might some of his warning signs be? _____

How intense might his warning signs be and how long might they last? _____

Scenario #3
"Kara worked very hard on a research paper. When she got her paper back, it had lots of red marks on it and the letter grade was a D."

What might seem threatening to Kara? _____

What might some of her warning signs be? _____

How intense might her warning signs be and how long might they last? _____

Scenario #4
"Charles was very close to his dog Spike. When he returned home from school one day, his Father told him that Spike had been hit by a car and was at the animal hospital."

What might seem threatening to Charles? _____

What might some of his warning signs be? _____

How intense might his warning signs be and how long might they last? _____

©YouthLight | 31

Section 3: Physical Strategies

Short Fuse

Purpose

Self-monitoring is a critical piece of Self-Regulation Training. When it comes to regulating our physical response to threat, awareness of the variables that impact how likely the system is to be triggered is key. There are several things that can increase the sensitivity of our alarm system. Gaining understanding of these variables can help us regulate our system to prevent problems from getting bigger. It also provides us an opportunity to let others know that we may need some space, or some time to lengthen our fuse.

This lesson is designed to increase the awareness of those variables that can shorten, or lengthen our fuse.

Note: It's helpful to have completed the Warning System lesson prior to starting this strategy.

Materials

- Short Fuse Worksheet, writing utensil, Piece of String and Scissors

Process

1. Using the string, explain that there are variables which seem to be related to how sensitive our warning System is at any given moment. Indicate that the string represents a fuse connected to your warning system. You might follow by saying something like:

    → "Sometimes it seems like our fuse is long, things happen around us, and our warning system isn't easily activated. Another way to say this is that sometimes we aren't easily threatened. Other times, it may seem like we are super-sensitive to the littlest things happening around us and our fuse is very short (cut the string to a very small length). It's important to realize those times when we are more sensitive so that we can do something about it. We may want to let others around us know that we need some time to ourselves."

2. Hand out the Short Fuse Worksheet and ask students to think about times when they've noticed feeling "on edge" or "irritable." Ask them to consider times when they've noticed that nothing seems to bother them.

3. Ask students to complete the worksheet.

4. Process using the Discussion Questions.

Section 3: Physical Strategies

Short Fuse (continued)

Discussion Questions

1. Have you ever given someone a warning to let them know that you need some time to yourself to relax? How did it go?

2. Were there themes that emerged from your answers to the questions on the worksheet? What are some key variables you can control to make your fuse longer more often?

3. What are some consequences of going through your day without recognizing your fuse is short?

4. What ideas did you come up with for lengthening your fuse?

Worksheet

Short Fuse

1. I've noticed that when I'm _____ my warning system seems to be more sensitive.

Fill in the blank with 5 possibilities:

1. _____
2. _____
3. _____
4. _____
5. _____

2. I've also noticed that when I _____, it seems to lengthen my fuse and I am able to tolerate and my warning system seems less sensitive.

Fill in the blank with 5 possibilities:

1. _____
2. _____
3. _____
4. _____
5. _____

Create a statement you can use to give others a polite warning that your "fuse" is short and you may need some time to fix it.

_____
_____
_____

Section 3: Physical Strategies

My Warning Signs

Purpose One of the first steps in diffusing emotional upset is successful recognition of our own personal physical changes that take place in the body. Although there are common signs, such as fist clenching and stomach upset, each person has their own individual specific signs that are unique. Many individuals are unaware of their own physical warning signs and they go undetected.

This lesson is designed to identify and clarify the physical signs of becoming upset. Upset can mean angry, sad, worried, etc. There are a number of ways to elicit the physical fight/flight/shut-down response. We experience this response, to certain degrees, several times per day.

Materials
- Warning Signs worksheet, writing utensil

Process

1. Provide a brief overview of the Fight/Flight/Shut-down system:

   "As human beings, we are equipped with an alarm system that responds when we feel threatened. When it is triggered, several things happen inside our bodies. Our bodies prepare to fight, run, or shut-down. Our heart-rate increases, chemicals are released, and the way our brain works changes. One interesting thing about this process is that it responds the same way to an emotional threat as it does to a physical threat. Another interesting thing that happens is that the thinking part of our brain doesn't work very well when our alarm is going off. Have you ever said something you didn't mean to someone you care about when you were upset? This explains how that can happen."

   Feel free to expand this description based on the audience.

2. Present the student with the worksheet and a writing utensil. Ask him/her to draw a full-body self-portrait in the space provided.

3. As he/she draws, discuss specific examples of changes that happen physically when people become upset. You can use a story to illustrate this process.

   For example, you may say, "Last week I was at the store and I was ready to check out. Just then, someone jumped in front of me in the check-out line. My alarm system was triggered because my brain must have seen this action as a threat. I remember feeling my face get hot and my stomach feeling upset. When I noticed these signs, I knew I was getting angry and needed to calm down before I did something I would feel bad about later."

Section 3: Physical Strategies

My Warning Signs (continued)

You may also give other examples of how emotional threats can trigger this system. Some examples include a break-up of a relationship, finding out you have a test tomorrow, or thinking about something unpleasant that happened to you in your past.

4. After the student completes the drawing, ask him/her to select warning signs that he/she has experienced from the list on the worksheet. Then ask the student to list any other signs that he/she has experienced that are not on the list in the extra spaces provided.

5. Ask students to think about common events that they may interpret as a threat and list them at the bottom of the page.

Variations

1. Group activity – Select a volunteer to deliver a short presentation on a random topic area. When the student completes the presentation, ask the student to describe any physical warning signs he/she noticed prior to, or during the presentation. Comment on any warning signs you were able to notice.

2. Select an age-appropriate video clip from YouTube™, or similar website, of a person becoming upset and identify the warning signs witnessed as a group.

Weekly Challenges

3. Ask students to watch a scary movie and take note of any physical warning signs they experience during the movie. Our warning signs can also be activated by seeing someone else in a threatening situation.

4. Over the next few days, take note of times when you experience warning signs. Also, pay attention to the warning signs of others. See how many times you experience this process in a single day.

Discussion Questions

1. How is this process related to success or failure in many areas of life?

2. If the thinking part of our brain isn't working well when our alarm is going off, what additional problems could that cause?

3. How do you turn off this alarm system? What things do we sometimes do that might keep it going?

4. Think about those who are close to you. What are their warning signs? How do you, or how could you, change what you do when others are experiencing their warning signs? Is it helpful?

Worksheet

My Warning Signs

Common Warning signs

1. Upset stomach
2. Headache
3. Clenched fists
4. Loud voice
5. Red face
6. Restless, fidgety, twitchy
7. Heart beating faster or louder
8. Sweaty palms
9. _____
10. _____

Draw Yourself Here

I sometimes feel threatened by:

_____
_____
_____
_____

©YouthLight | 37

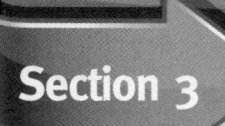

Physical Strategies

Create a Safe Place

Purpose One of the most common reasons for reactivity is feeling threatened. Our alarm system can be triggered by a perceived physical threat or a perceived emotional threat. Our alarm system will operate in the same way to each type of threat. Additionally, individuals who have experienced trauma may operate in a constant state of alarm. The cure for feeling threatened is to create a feeling of safety. To gain insight into our own ability to generate feelings of threat and also to create calm feelings of safety is empowering. This activity is designed to help individuals develop a plan to create a sense of safety when they need it.

Materials A Safe Place handout, Paper and Drawing utensils

Process

1. Begin by discussing the terms "threat" and "safe." You can use the following script to start the discussion:

   → "Today we are going to think about what the words "threat" and "safe" mean to us. When we feel threatened, our alarm system will sound. It will feel the same whether we are being chased by a tiger, or if someone calls us a name. Our body responds the same to physical threats as it does to emotional threats. Today, we are going to develop a plan for creating a sense of safety to shut down our alarm system. When we are safe, we feel relaxed and calm. We are not thinking about what's bothering us, or worrying about anything that's happened in the past, or will happen next."

2. Feel free to look up the word on the Internet, or in a dictionary together.

3. Present the handout and complete Number 1 together. Discuss the personal meaning of the word safe and what items may help to create a sense of safety.

*Note: Be mindful that teenagers who have experienced trauma may not see the same level of safety in the common places that you may describe (i.e. – home, bedroom, etc.)

4. Move on to Number 2 and identify things that may not be helpful in creating a sense of safety. For example, if one continues to think about the threatening situation, the alarm system will continue to be triggered.

5. Help the individual visualize himself/herself in their own safe place and draw it in the box on the handout.

6. Discuss specific things that help the teen feel safe in his/her Safe Place.

Section 3: Physical Strategies

Create a Safe Place... (CONTINUED)

Variations
1. Small Group – Have a small group of teens complete the handout and share/process their answers together supportively.
2. Situational – Identify a specific place or time when the individual is noticeably struggling with feeling unsafe. Alter the exercise so that it applies to only the specific situation.
3. Generate a group discussion about how to create a feeling of safety in places like school, the community, etc.

Discussion Questions
1. What are some examples of when you could have used your Safe Place this past week?
2. What items can you put in your Safe Place to help you take your mind off of what you are upset about?
3. It's important to get to your Safe Place before you react to the situation. What can you do to help yourself remember to use your Safe Place and use it quickly?

Worksheet

Create a Safe Place

1. Things that help you feel safe:

   _____
   _____
   _____

2. Things that aren't helpful in your safe place:

   _____
   _____
   _____

What Does Your Safe Place Look Like?

Section 3: Physical Strategies

Mobile Safety

Purpose

The ability to shut down our physical alarm system depends on how successful we are at creating a sense of safety. In the Create a Safe Place activity, we developed a place and a plan to create this feeling. However, there are many times that we experience a threatening situation and we are not able to get to our safe place immediately.

This activity is designed to give individuals the ability to create a sense of safety wherever they are and whenever they need it.

Materials

- Safety Script, Comfortable Area

Process

1. Discuss the idea that a simple way to shut down our warning system is to create a sense of safety. The cure for feeling threatened is safety.

2. Explain that this activity is designed to give individuals the ability to create a sense of safety wherever they are and whenever they need it. The more one practices, the more effective this skill will become.

3. Reduce the lighting in the room and read the script aloud at a slow, relaxing pace.

4. After completing the script, process the experience with participants.

Variation

1. Combine soothing music or sounds with the script to create an even more relaxing environment.

Discussion Questions

1. What changes did you notice in your body when you compare how you felt at the beginning of the exercise with how you felt at the end?

2. Discuss how you could practice using a calming technique like this one three times per week. What are the challenges? What are the benefits?

Worksheet

Safety Script

"Get into a comfortable position and close your eyes. Now take a few slow, deep breaths. Feel the air move in and out of your lungs. You may have felt some of your body's warning signs earlier in the day. It's normal to have times when we feel upset and where our heart beats faster and our muscles feel tight. But right now, we are going to let all of that go. As you continue to breathe deeply, take a moment to scan your body for any warning signs or tension that may still be there. Notice the tension and discomfort… and then let if fade away as you take another slow deep breath and let it out.

Now, imagine that you are standing at the top of a stairway. At the bottom of the stairway is a door. There are five steps and as you go down each step, you will feel more and more relaxed. Let's count backward from five to zero as you walk slowly down the stairs. Five…your feet and legs feel heavy and relaxed, four…your back and stomach feel calm and relaxed, three…your chest feels calm and relaxed as you take slow deep breaths, two…your hands, arms and shoulders feel loose and relaxed, one…your neck, face and head feel loose and relaxed. Zero…you have reached the door, leaving all of your tension behind you. The door in front of you leads to a place where you have total control. It's safe because you are the master there. Use your secret password to enter the door (If this is the first time you've heard this, then create a password for yourself. You may want to choose a word like CALM or SAFE for your password). Now, visualize the door opening and imagine yourself walking into your safe place.

This place is full of things that help you to feel Calm and Safe. You are happy here. Continue to take slow deep breaths as you explore your Safe Place. You can spend time creating whatever you like here, or just relaxing.

Notice the colors and the sounds of your safe place… Here, you feel comfortable, calm and relaxed. Remember to take long, slow, deep breaths as you explore the sights, sounds and feelings of your safe place.

Now, picture the word "SAFE." The letters "S," "A," "F," "E" may be written in the clouds, or the trees, or on the walls of your safe place. Repeat the word to yourself in your mind… "SAFE." Notice this deep feeling of safety and calm that you feel right now as you picture the word "SAFE." After you have practiced this exercise a few times, you will simply be able to close your eyes and say the word "SAFE" to yourself and immediately your body will begin to feel more calm and relaxed.

Now it's time to come back from your safe place. Remember that you can come back to this place of Safety and Calm anytime you like. It's always here, waiting to welcome you. Picture the door that leads out of your safe place. Open the door and notice how peaceful you feel. Carry this sense of peace and happiness with you as we move back up the five stairs. One…take a slow, deep breath, two…still feeling calm and safe, three…becoming more awake with positive energy, four….remembering that you can come back to your safe place any time you like, five…open your eyes feeling safe and wide awake."

Section 3: Physical Strategies

Stretching and Movement

Purpose Patterned, rhythmic activities increase our sense of safety by creating predictability. Smooth, relaxing physical movements are a simple way to create a sense of safety and calmness. Repetitive movements and stretching combined with slow deep breaths provide a powerful way to prevent our alarm system from becoming activated. These techniques can be used as a preventative strategy to "lengthen our fuse" or they can be implemented in response to a stressful situation to stop further escalation of our warning signs.

Many of these stretches and movements are adapted from Qigong and Yoga.

Materials
- Stretching and Movement Guide

Process
1. Introduce this activity by relating stretching and movement to the idea of patterns and predictability. You may say something like:

    → "Today, we are going to practice some simple movements that you can use to create a sense of safety and calm. Repetitive movements, combined with calm breathing send a strong message to the body that you are safe. There are also many other benefits gained from movement and stretching. Many studies have shown that these types of simple activities can reduce stress, increase positive moods, decrease physical pain, reduce the risk of serious illness, and much more. We will be learning how to do some basic movements and stretches, similar to those in Qigong and Yoga."

2. Ask participants to stand up and spread out to give everyone enough space to move.

3. Use the Stretching and Movement Guide to lead the individual(s) through the motions.

4. Remind participants to focus on taking slow, deep breaths and to move slowly/smoothly through motions.

Discussion Questions
1. How did you feel while doing the movements?
2. How could you incorporate this practice into your daily or weekly routine?
3. How do you think this experience relates to the calming effects created by things that are patterned, rhythmic, and repetitive?

Worksheet

Stretching and Movement Guide

Movement #1 – "The Wave"

Step 1 – Inhale as you raise your arms up in-front of you to shoulder-height, keeping your wrists loose.

Step 2 – Exhale as you lower your arms back down to your sides, bending your knees slightly at the bottom of the move. Bend your wrists to raise your hands upward, while your arms are moving downward.

Step 3 – Repeat 8 – 12 times.

Movement #2 – "The Push"

Step 1 – Imagine that you are standing in water up to your shoulders. Place your right foot forward. Inhale, and as you exhale, create a pushing motion with your arms toward the front as if you are attempting to push the water away from you. As you push forward, gently shift your weight forward to your right foot, while being careful to maintain balance.

Step 2 – Inhale as you draw your arms back toward your body as if you are pulling water back in your direction. Gently shift your weight back to your left foot.

Step 3 – Repeat this motion 8 – 12 times, switch positions to have your left foot forward and repeat 8 – 12 times.

Movement #3 – "The Gathering"

Step 1 – Place your right foot slightly forward. Inhale as you bend down and move your hands in a crossing motion out in front of you as if you were gathering something.

Step 2 – Exhale as you stand and raise hands above your head, uncrossing your hands as if releasing what you've gathered into the air.

Step 3 - Repeat this motion 8 – 12 times, switch positions to have your left foot forward and repeat 8 – 12 times.

Movement #4 – "The Puppet"

Step 1 – Imagine that one string is connecting your right hand to your left knee and another string is connecting your left hand to your right knee.

Step 2 – As you inhale, raise your right hand and your left knee as if they are connected. Lower them slowly as you exhale. Inhale and raise your left hand and your right knee as if they are connected. Lower them slowly as you exhale.

Step 3 – Repeat 8 – 12 times.

Worksheet

Stretching and Movement Guide...(CONTINUED)

Stretch #1 – "The Meow Mooo"

Step 1 – Begin on all fours with your back parallel to the floor.

Step 2 – As you inhale, attempt to raise your back toward the ceiling, gently arching upward similar to the way a cat arches its back.

Step 3 – As you exhale, allow your stomach and chest to sink down below parallel toward the floor, similar to the way a cow might appear to be standing.

Step 4 – Slowly repeat alternating between these two positions 8 – 12 times.

Stretch #2 – "Reach for the Sky"

Step 1 – Stand with your feet shoulder width apart and balanced.

Step 2 – Inhale as you raise your arms up slowly up over your head as if reaching for the sky creating a healthy, balanced stretch.

Step 3 – Exhale as you slowly lower your arms back to your sides.

Step 4 – Repeat this motion 8 – 12 times.

Stretch #3 – "The Fold"

Step 1 – Stand with your feet shoulder width apart and balanced.

Step 2 – Inhale, and as you exhale, slowly bend at the waist reaching your hands toward the floor as far as you need to for a good stretch.

Step 3 – Inhale as you slowly straighten back up to a standing position.

Step 4 – Repeat this motion 8 – 12 times.

Stretch #4 – "Side Bend"

Step 1 - Stand with your feet shoulder width apart and balanced with your hands at your sides.

Step 2 – As you inhale, bend at the waist leaning slightly to the left while extending your right arm over your head.

Step 3 – Exhale as you return to a balanced position with your hands at your sides.

Step 4 – As you inhale, bend at the waist leaning slightly to the right while extending your left arm over your head.

Step 5 – Repeat these steps 8 – 12 times.

Note: Search Qigong and Yoga for more information and additional stretches/movements.

Section 3: Physical Strategies

Take Advantage of the Senses

Purpose — Just as our senses are useful in detecting threats, they can also be used to create a sense of safety to help de-activate our alarm system. For example, certain scents have been shown to help create feelings of relaxation. Additionally, music can have a calming effect on the mind and body. Gaining an understanding of what sounds, sights, smells, and objects help us feel calm can provide a useful way to shut down our warning system by creating an environment that seems familiar (predictable) and soothing.

Materials
- Senses Worksheet, simple items from around the house (Examples – candles, spices, flowers, homemade quilt, pictures)

Process

1. Gather several items from around the house that may help individuals feel calm and safe. Include different fragrances, pictures, music, and tactile objects. Be creative. You may want to use the Internet for additional ideas.

2. Introduce this lesson by saying something like:

    "Threats are first detected by our senses. This can trigger our alarm system and lead to feelings of anger, sadness, and anxiety. However, we can also use our senses to help shut down the alarm system by surrounding ourselves with items that our senses interpret as calming or soothing. Today, we are going to identify some items that we can use to create a feeling of safety when we need to. This is usually a very individualized process. We each have a unique perception of what helps us to feel calm and safe. We are going to experience several different items to see which items help us feel calm and safe."

3. Pass around the items you brought to the lesson. Generate discussion about each item and how it may be used to enhance a "safe place." Many of these items can trigger memories of a time where individuals felt safe and calm

4. Individuals can use the Senses worksheet to write down items the help create a calming effect. They may also want to indicate items to avoid when trying to create a calm/safe environment.

Note: Keep in mind that certain items may also trigger memories of unpleasant events. It's important to also identify those types of items, but be aware of individual comments and responses as items are passed around and discussed.

Section 3: Physical Strategies

Take Advantage of the Senses... (CONTINUED)

Discussion Questions

1. What do you think about how the sense of "taste" is related to calm feelings? What are your thoughts about using food as a calming and comforting item?

2. Are there certain objects you take with you, or could carry with you, that may help create a feeling of safety when you need it?

3. Are there other unhealthy, less helpful habits, you currently engage in to self-soothe that could be replaced by using the items identified in this activity?

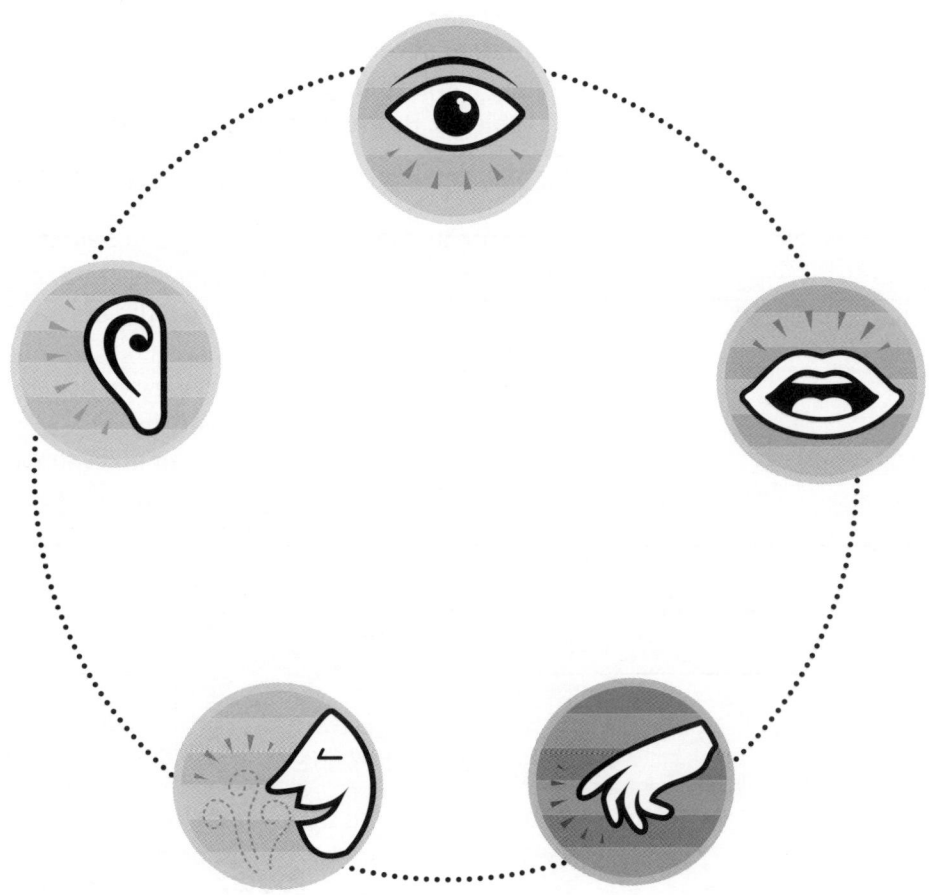

Senses

Worksheet

Identify items that you find to have a calming effect in each of the areas below. Also, identify those items that seem to have the opposite effect.

Calming   **Alarming**

Sights

_____ _____
_____ _____
_____ _____

Sounds

_____ _____
_____ _____
_____ _____

Scents

_____ _____
_____ _____
_____ _____

Touch

_____ _____
_____ _____
_____ _____

Section 3: Physical Strategies

Routines and Predictability

Purpose As we've mentioned in previous lessons, regulating our physical response to perceived threats is an important first step in developing healthy self-regulatory skills. As human beings, our bodies tend to perform well when we feel safe. Learning to create predictability in our lives can be a very powerful skill to create a sense of safety. Additionally, in times of transition, change, or turmoil, predictable routines and patterns can help to off-set our physical stress response.

This lesson is designed to raise awareness regarding the power of creating, and keeping, a fairly regular routine.

Materials
- Daily Routine Worksheet, writing utensil

Process
1. Explain, or review, the connection between predictability and a sense of safety/performance. You might say:

   → "We tend to feel better and perform better when we feel safe and calm. We feel more safe and calm when the things around us are predictable. Since we can't control many of the things around us, we must focus on where we can create predictability. One simple way to create some predictability in our lives is to maintain a fairly consistent daily routine. Today we are going to take a few minutes to look at our existing routine and clarify it a little."

2. As you hand out the schedule, share some examples of some of the tasks from your own daily routine. You may point out how it is fairly constant, but it's also flexible. We don't want our schedule to be a source of stress. Its purpose is to help provide some predictable structure, but we must also be able to flex with real life.

3. Ask students to complete the schedule for all seven days. Be sure to emphasize things like regular meal times, consistent bed-times, and "wake-up" times. Also mention that it's a good idea to include both work and leisure times.

4. Ask the students to use this schedule for 3 weeks and then meet to reflect on the process.

Variation
1. Instead of, or in addition to, the paper worksheet ask students to create the schedule on a chosen electronic device (e.g. – phone, tablet, etc.). Explore alerts and alarm features and how those can be useful.

Section 3: Physical Strategies

Routines and Predictability...(CONTINUED)

Discussion Questions

1. What are the positives of keeping a fairly regular schedule?

2. What changes do you notice in your mood, or behavior, when you are "off" of your schedule?

3. Most of the successful systems in our world operate on cycles. How do you think this exercise on routines is related?

Worksheet

*Routines and Predictability
Daily Routine*

Time	Monday	Tuesday	Wednesday	Thursday	Friday	Saturday	Sunday

Section 3: Physical Strategies

Physical Regulation Review for Mastery

Purpose — As individuals move through the Self-Regulation training system, it's important to take time to review and reflect on the skills they have learned to move toward mastery. This lesson can be used as a review of the 3 Skill-training areas of Physical Regulation:

- Identification of physical warning signs for upset
- Learning how to get safe to deactivate the warning system
- Learn and implement calming skills

Materials — Physical Regulation Review, writing utensil

Process

1. Explain that the student(s) have completed the first section of Self-Regulation Training. Refer back to the "Keys to My Success" if you are using this as a guide for your curriculum.

2. As you hand out the Physical Regulation Review, ask them to complete the short activities to ensure that they have a good understanding of these important skills.

3. Come back together and discuss the results and complete the Optional Activities if time allows.

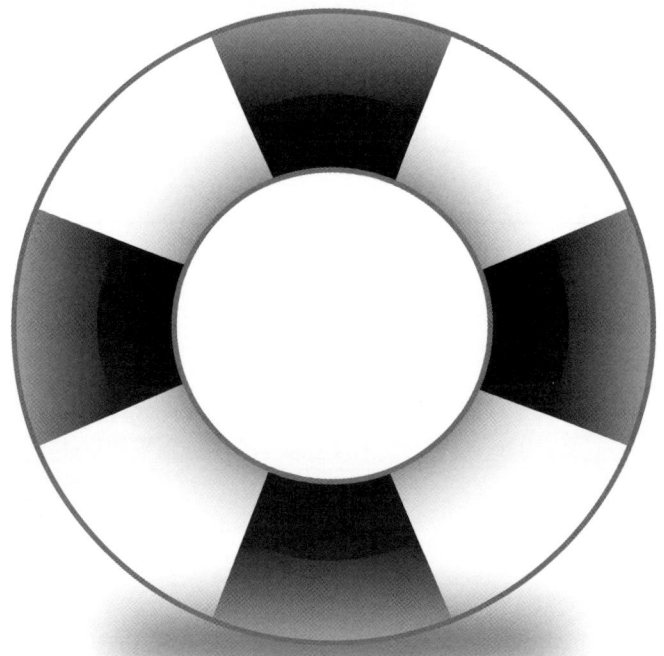

Worksheet

Physical Regulation Review

Word Bank	Heart Beating Faster	Warning Signs
	Predictability	Earlier

Fill in the blank – Use the word bank for the first four.

1. When we feel threatened, we experience _____ in our body.

2. One way to help shut-down our Warning System is to create a sense of _____ .

3. _____ is an example of a physical warning sign.

4. The _____ you notice your warning signs, the easier it is to shut down the warning system.

5. My favorite calming activity is _____ .

Read the scenarios and answer the questions.

Scenario #1
Dillon has a final exam in the morning. He just found out that he has to work late tonight.

Name three physical warning signs Dillon might be experiencing:

1. _____
2. _____
3. _____

Identify two healthy ways he could shut down his warning system:

1. _____
2. _____

Scenario #2
Krista just overheard a conversation between a group of girls she thought were her friends. They were making very hurtful comments about her.

Name three physical warning signs Krista might be experiencing:

1. _____
2. _____
3. _____

Identify two healthy ways she could shut down her warning system:

1. _____
2. _____

Worksheet

# Physical Regulation Review
...(CONTINUED)

Optional Activities and Discussion:

1. Demonstrate a healthy calming exercise (relaxation exercise, stretching, patterned movement, etc.).

2. Describe how calming exercises, or patterned and repetitive motions, can be used in a preventative way to keep our warning system at a low level of activation.

3. Name as many Physical Warning Signs as you can.

4. Discuss how warning signs are similar, or different, for anger, worry, and sadness.
   Discuss how you are able to create a "safe place" in your mind when you are not able to physically leave a situation.

5. Create and perform a short skit where something happens to trigger the threat response. Point out the warning signs along the way and the skills utilized to shut down the warning system successfully.

Section 4: Emotional Strategies

Emotional Strategies

The second phase of Self-Regulation requires the skills to label emotions accurately and express them in healthy ways. In addition to these two skills, strategies contained in this section also address the concept of emotional control. It is important for an individual to understand that he/she has the ability to control and moderate the expression of his/her emotions.

To increase the chance of success, be sure that you have addressed physical regulation skills before getting too far into the emotional regulation skills. Additionally, we do not recommend attempting to implement the emotional strategies when the individual is experiencing physical warning signs. These strategies were designed to be utilized when a person is physically calm. If they are physically upset, first use a physical strategy to help them return to a calm baseline.

The following interventions are designed to teach the basic skills of emotional regulation. There are three main functional skill-training areas within the Emotional Regulation domain:

- Identification of basic emotions
- Learn/Practice healthy ways to express emotions
- Understand/Believe that we own our emotions and are responsible for them; other people and events have no control over our emotions unless we allow it

Section 4: Emotional Strategies

What's Your Status

Purpose An important step in helping individuals become better at regulating emotions is being able to identify emotions accurately. This skill can help provide some clarity and direction in a time of confusion and turmoil. The following strategy is designed to teach individuals how to accurately identify, express, and discuss emotions.

Materials
- What's Your Status Worksheet, writing utensil

Process
1. Emotions are part of our everyday lives, yet, sometimes we seem to know very little about them. Also, some emotions can be very strong, seem confusing, and can be difficult to deal with. One way to improve our chances of success in dealing with emotions is to be able to label them correctly.

2. As you hand out the worksheet, explain that one of the first steps in solving a problem is to know exactly what the issue is. If you are able to accurately label the emotion, you will have a better chance of knowing how to "fix" it.

3. Discuss the concept of emoticons (i.e. – text symbols used to indicate emotions) as a way people try to express how they might be feeling.

4. Ask students to complete the worksheet.

Variation
1. Ask students to share a real example of a message they recently sent or received and ask others to guess how the individual may have been feeling at the time.

Discussion Questions
1. What might be your reply to the person in each of the examples?
2. What are your thoughts about using emoticons? What are the pros and cons?
3. Other than emoticons, what are some signs to indicate how a person may be feeling?

Worksheet

What's Your Status?

Read each status update, name the emotion(s) the individual may be feeling, draw the emoticon (example – :(means sad) , and rate how intense the feeling might be.

1. *"paper due tomorrow and my laptop just died"*

   Emotion(s)   Draw Emoticon   Intensity (1-10)

   _____   _____   _____

2. *"Just made the dance team"*

   Emotion(s)   Draw Emoticon   Intensity (1-10)

   _____   _____   _____

3. *"guess I'll be the only one going to the dance by myself"*

   Emotion(s)   Draw Emoticon   Intensity (1-10)

   _____   _____   _____

4. *"seems like nothing I do today is working out"*

   Emotion(s)   Draw Emoticon   Intensity (1-10)

   _____   _____   _____

5. *"done feeling like I'm not good enough for you"*

   Emotion(s)   Draw Emoticon   Intensity (1-10)

   _____   _____   _____

6. *"omg... I think my parents have been reading my messages"*

   Emotion(s)   Draw Emoticon   Intensity (1-10)

   _____   _____   _____

Section 4: Emotional Strategies

Feelings Playlist

Purpose — Healthy emotional regulation requires the ability to identify and express emotions in healthy ways. This activity is designed to help individuals develop and practice the skills needed to accurately identify, connect with, and express their feelings. This strategy also provides an example of how music can impact our feelings and provide us with a healthy way to express emotions.

Materials
- Feelings Playlist Worksheet, writing utensil

Process

1. Explain that there are healthy and unhealthy ways to express emotions like anger, sadness, and worry. You may say:

    "Understanding our feelings and how to express them can impact our ability to be successful socially, academically, on the playing field, on the job and many other areas of our lives. We've often heard many ways how not to express our feelings, but we rarely are taught, or get to practice, healthy ways to express them."

2. As you hand out the worksheet, explain that music has long been used as an outlet for emotions. We play, sing, and write about our experiences, and listen to the experiences of others through music. Music is also a patterned, rhythmic experience for us (link back to physical regulation and the importance of this concept).

3. Ask the students to think about the music they listen to and how it can be used to express, or connect with emotions they experience.

4. Ask the students to complete the Feelings Playlist worksheet.

Variation

1. Incorporate the use of technology. There are several Apps and programs that can help you build a playlist to match how you are feeling. Use a phone, tablet, or computer to explore these programs as a group. Discuss their features and how they may be helpful for emotional regulation.

Discussion Questions

1. What role has music played in your life and how you express, or connect with emotions?

2. How can music have an impact on our emotions?

Section 4: Emotional Strategies

Feelings Playlist...(CONTINUED)

3. As you share your Playlists, are there themes to the music identified by different individuals and how different types of music relate to different emotions?

4. Discuss how music can be used to help change your mood, or how the music can help you stay with a particular mood to work through it?

Worksheet

Feelings Playlist

List songs that you can use to express or connect with healthy expression of each of the different emotions.

Happy/Excited

_____
_____
_____

Worried

_____
_____
_____

Angry

_____
_____
_____

Sad

_____
_____
_____

Lonely

_____
_____
_____

Loss/Grief

_____
_____
_____

Section 4: Emotional Strategies

Sticky Feelings

Purpose — Those who struggle with Self-Regulation tend to have difficulty identifying and expressing emotions in healthy ways. This simple exercise is designed to help individuals practice both identification and expression of emotions.

Materials
- Six pieces of poster board, one or two packages of sticky notes

Process
1. Write one of the following feelings on each of the poster boards and hang them on the wall in different areas of the room.
2. Angry, Sad, Worried, Happy, Lonely, Disappointed
3. Explain that emotions can be difficult to identify. We are much more likely to be able to express our feelings in healthy ways if we can accurately identify them.
4. Provide each student with at least six sticky notes.
5. Ask them to write down a recent example of when they felt each of the six emotions on the sticky notes and place it on the corresponding poster. There is no need for them to put their name on their items.
6. When everyone is finished, read through the sticky notes one feeling at a time.

Discussion Questions
1. What are some common themes that emerged for each of the feelings?
2. What's the difference between sad, lonely and disappointed?
3. Discuss how anger is often described as a "secondary emotion." This means that it is said to be accompanied by another emotion that may be "underneath" the anger.
4. Name as many other emotions as you can.

Section 4: Emotional Strategies

Emotional Build-Up

Purpose — Individuals struggling with Self-Regulation often let their emotions build up inside them to a level that becomes impossible to contain. They reach a point where the emotions burst out in ways that can be destructive or harmful. This strategy is designed to illustrate how emotions that are "stuffed" away can build up, become very heavy and/or come bursting out.

Materials
- Two bottles of water, Story of Alex's Day

Process

1. Begin by asking a student to volunteer for a quick demonstration. Hold out the two bottles of water and ask the participants how heavy they believe the bottles to be. Most generally, they will say the bottles are fairly light (one or two pounds).

2. Ask the volunteer to hold one bottle of water in each hand and lift his/her arms straight out from their sides and up to shoulder height. Ask them to remain in this position.

3. While the volunteer continues to hold the water, provide a brief overview of how emotions can build up inside of us. You might say something like:

    → "Emotions that are not expressed will continue to build up. Similar to a volcano, they can continue to build until they come bursting out. Stuffing our feelings, or pretending they are not there, can cause them to build-up inside of us and become very, very heavy to carry around."

    → *Check on your volunteer to see if he/she is still doing okay and ask if the water is getting heavier. If so, continue on.

    → "It's important to learn how to express your feelings in healthy ways so that they don't continue to build up and explode, or wear you down on the inside."

4. Now, ask the volunteer to set the bottles down. Ask the volunteer if the water seemed to get heavier. Connect this demonstration to the idea of emotions building up and becoming heavier. After a moment, ask the volunteer to pick the bottles up again and compare how light they feel now versus how heavy they felt when he/she set them down a moment ago.

5. Draw a connection between setting the bottles down for a moment and using your Safe Place, or expressing the feelings to "lighten the load." Then when you come back to the issue, it doesn't seem so "heavy."

6. Read the Story of Alex's Day individually, or as a group. Process the discussion questions.

Worksheet

Story of Alex's Rough Day

Alex didn't sleep very well last night because he was worrying about an argument he had with his friend Rebecca. He didn't hear his alarm and had to rush to get ready to leave for school. On the way to school, Alex's older brother Sam was making comments about how he was so much better at everything than Alex. Alex felt his face getting red and his heart beginning to beat faster. When Alex got to school, he realized that he had forgotten his assignment for his third-hour class. He didn't say anything to the teacher and had nothing to turn in that day. At lunch, Alex dropped his tray and the food went all over his clothes. People were laughing. Alex turned red and stomped out of the lunch room. By afternoon, his stomach was turning and his head began to hurt. He felt like things were building up inside.

At home later that evening, Alex walked into the kitchen, and as he approached, he heard his sister completing the last part of a sentence. He heard, "… and he's acting like a total jerk!" Alex slammed his phone on the ground. It broke into several pieces. As he stormed away, he yelled, "Everything and everyone is against me! I hate all of you!" Alex's sister was actually talking about how her boyfriend had been acting lately.

Story of Alex's Better Day

Alex couldn't get to sleep last night because he was worrying about an argument he had with his friend Rebecca. He decided to get up and talk with his Mother about the fight. Talking about it helped him come up with a plan to fix things with Rebecca. He had a good night sleep and woke up for school on time. On the way to school, Alex's older brother Sam was making comments about how he was so much better at everything than Alex. Alex felt his face getting red and his heart beginning to beat faster. He took a few deep breaths, and then said, "I don't like it when Sam says I'm not very good at things. I do my best, and that's what matters." When Alex got to school, he realized that he had forgotten his assignment for his third-hour class. He apologized and let his teacher know that he had completed the assignment, but forgot to bring it today. He asked if he could turn it in first thing the next morning and the teacher agreed. At lunch, Alex dropped his tray and the food went all over his clothes. People were laughing. Alex started to turn red, but then he took a deep breath and realized that it was funny and he laughed at himself too. By afternoon, Alex realized he was having quite a day. He took a few moments to close his eyes and clear his mind. He imagined himself in a safe place and decided he could take this feeling with him for the rest of the day.

At home later that evening, Alex walked into the kitchen, and as he approached, he heard his sister completing the last part of a sentence. He heard, "… and he's acting like a total jerk!" Alex asked, "Who are you talking about?" His sister said, "I'm talking about how my boyfriend seems to just go off at the smallest things and can seem like a real jerk sometimes." Alex smiled and said, "Maybe I can give him a few tips on how to manage that a little better."

Section 4: Emotional Strategies

Emotional Build-Up... (CONTINUED)

Discussion Questions

1. What was the same in both stories?

2. What was different in the two stories?

3. What skills did Alex use in the second story?

4. Alex wasn't able to control the problems happening around him, but what could he control?

5. What is it that determines how you respond to difficult situations that happen around you?

Section 4: Emotional Strategies

Advice Blog

Purpose — Accurate identification of emotions is an important skill in developing Self-Regulation. Equally important are the skills related to healthy expression of those emotions. Similar to a magazine advice column with stories troubling teenagers, this exercise challenges participants to help other teenagers struggling with emotional situations described in short scenarios.

Materials
- Advice Blog Worksheet, writing utensil

Process
1. Explain the importance of accurate identification of feelings. Communicate how much easier a problem is to solve when you can identify, label and sort out the pieces.
2. Also discuss how true it is that we often give very good advice to others, but sometimes we don't apply those same solutions to our own lives.
3. As you hand out the worksheet, indicate that the participants are now advice columnists for a Teen Blog Website. Teenagers write-in with problems asking for advice.
4. The task is to read the short scenarios, identify the feelings, and communicate a healthy way for the individual to express those feelings.

Discussion Questions
1. What are some examples of times when you were able to give good advice to someone else? Who do you go to for advice and why?
2. Why do you think we are often able to give good advice to others, but don't apply that good information to our own problems?
3. What's the difference between healthy and unhealthy ways of expressing emotions? Use examples.

Variation — For small groups, ask each group to write their own problem story for the advice column related to an emotion. Next, each group passes their problem story to another group. Each group works to identify the emotion(s) in the problem story and writes a helpful response including healthy ways to express the identified emotion. Share the results for discussion.

Worksheet

Jessica
"It seems like wherever I go, I don't fit in. People don't understand me. I'm not like everyone else and I don't want to be like everyone else. People just don't get it… and they don't get me. Please help."

It sounds like you are feeling: _____

Here are some ways you might be able to express that emotion so you can feel better:

_____
_____

Chloe
"My sister and I look very much the same. People have always said we could be twins, but she is head cheerleader, has lots of friends and gets straight A's. I am creative on the inside and like to spend time by myself. I really don't enjoy big crowds and am not athletic. I'm kind of awkward and sometimes I wish I was more like her. Please help."

It sounds like you are feeling: _____

Here are some ways you might be able to express that emotion so you can feel better:

_____
_____

Tiana
"My parents are always arguing. It seems like my house is a war zone. Sometimes I can't sleep. I just lay there and think about what might happen. I wonder if other people know how messed up my family really is. Please help."

It sounds like you are feeling: _____

Here are some ways you might be able to express that emotion so you can feel better:

_____
_____

Jake
"These guys at school are always hounding me. It seems like whatever I do, they can find a way to make me look stupid in front of everyone. Don't they have anything better to do than make my life miserable? Please help."

It sounds like you are feeling: _____

Here are some ways you might be able to express that emotion so you can feel better:

_____
_____

Advice Blog ...(CONTINUED)

Worksheet

Tiffany
"*My best friend, or maybe I should say ex-best friend, totally made a move on the boy I like. I've liked him forever... and she knew that. Please help.*"

It sounds like you are feeling: _____

Here are some ways you might be able to express that emotion so you can feel better:

_____

_____

Lynn
"*I get up early to help my little brother and sister get ready for school. Fix everyone breakfast. Work hard for good grades all day. Go to practice after school. Hurry home for dinner. Do homework until late at night and take a shower if I'm lucky to have enough time to get in the bathroom before someone does. Now I'm thinking I will have to get a job if I want to get a car. When is there time to do what I want? Please help.*"

It sounds like you are feeling: _____

Here are some ways you might be able to express that emotion so you can feel better:

_____

_____

Sebastian
"*My best friend is going through a hard time. He's changed a lot since grade school and he's into some stuff that I don't really want to be part of. I'm sure his parents don't know about it and I'm starting to wonder if we can still be friends. Please help.*"

It sounds like you are feeling: _____

Here are some ways you might be able to express that emotion so you can feel better:

_____

_____

Section 4: Emotional Strategies

Top 10 List for Healthy Expression

Purpose
After learning to accurately identify emotions, the next step is to teach healthy ways for those emotions to be expressed. We often hear many ways "not" to express emotions such as anger, but when do we teach individuals how to appropriately express feelings of anger, worry, and sadness? This activity is designed to help individuals generate several healthy avenues, or outlets, for their emotions.

Materials
- Top 10 List for Healthy Expression Worksheet, writing utensil

Process
1. Explain that we often assume that people know how to express their feelings, but learning to express them in healthy ways is a skill. Emotions are like energy. If we don't have healthy outlets for them, they can fester inside, or come bursting out.
2. As you hand out the worksheet, explain that this exercise is similar to other "Top 10 Lists" they've probably seen before.
3. The task is to identify at least 2 unique feelings and generate healthy outlets, or ways to express those feelings.
4. To have a complete Top 10 List, they must complete all 10.

Discussion Questions
1. How many times do you think you've been told how "not" to express an emotion, or the way you did express an emotion was inappropriate? When have you been given a lesson on how to appropriately express a feeling?
2. Feelings like anger and worry are a normal part of our daily lives. How could not using healthy expression of emotions impact your life in a negative way?
3. What are some good examples of how other people you know express emotions in healthy ways? Or unhealthy ways?

Worksheet

Top 10 List For Healthy Expression

What you can do: **Feeling**

1. _____   _____

2. _____   _____

3. _____   _____

4. _____   _____

5. _____   _____

6. _____   _____

7. _____   _____

8. _____   _____

9. _____   _____

10. _____   _____

Section 4: Emotional Strategies

Healthy Expression Skits

Purpose
Learning to express emotions in healthy ways takes practice. Sharing our feelings with others can be difficult at times, and emotions are sometimes challenging to explain and cope with. This activity is designed to help individuals practice healthy strategies for expressing emotions, as well as identify unhealthy forms of expression.

Materials
- Healthy Expression Skit Worksheet, writing utensil

Process

1. Divide up into groups. Explain to the groups that emotions are a normal part of our daily lives, but the way we choose to express those emotions can impact our chances of success in many areas of life. It's also directly related to how happy we will be in the long run.

2. As you hand out the Healthy Expression Skit worksheet, let the groups know that they will have a few minutes to use the worksheet to create skits that will be performed in-front of the larger group.

3. First, they will perform the skit with the unhealthy expression ending. Encourage them to take the story through to the consequences of this action.

4. Next, they will perform the skit with the healthy ending.

5. Process the discussion questions as a large group.

Discussion Questions

1. Were there any themes that arose out of the healthy and unhealthy expression endings?

2. How can unhealthy expression of emotions lead to failure socially, emotionally, academically, on the job, in relationships, in sports, and in other areas of life?

3. If you've had some training in warning signs, did you observe any warning signs in the skits? Any calming strategies?

Healthy Expression Skit

Worksheet

What's the Problem?
_____
_____

What's the Feeling?
_____

Where is this taking place?
_____

Who are the characters?
_____

Unhealthy Expression Script
_____
_____
_____
_____

Healthy Expression Script
_____
_____
_____
_____

Section 4: Emotional Strategies

Expression Style Quiz

Purpose Those who regulate poorly often struggle to find healthy outlets for their emotions. This brief lesson helps to bring those activities into awareness and can help to clarify healthy expressive strategies the individual may already enjoy. It may also open new doors for different healthy outlets.

Materials
- Expression Style Quiz, writing utensil

Process
1. Explain the importance of having healthy outlets for our emotions. Emotions will come out in healthy or unhealthy ways, depending upon how we choose to express them.

2. As you hand out the Expression Style Quiz, share some of your own healthy expressive outlets. Explain that each of us may develop our own unique way of expressing our feelings. The main issue is that these emotions will come out in one form or another, and those who find healthy outlets will be able to avoid significant emotional issues that could impact relationships, their own health, and ability to be successful.

3. Ask the students to complete the quiz, score it, and process their results.

Discussion Questions
1. What healthy outlets do others who are close to you tend to use?
2. Name five unhealthy ways for emotions to be expressed?
3. What can happen if we "stuff" our emotions?

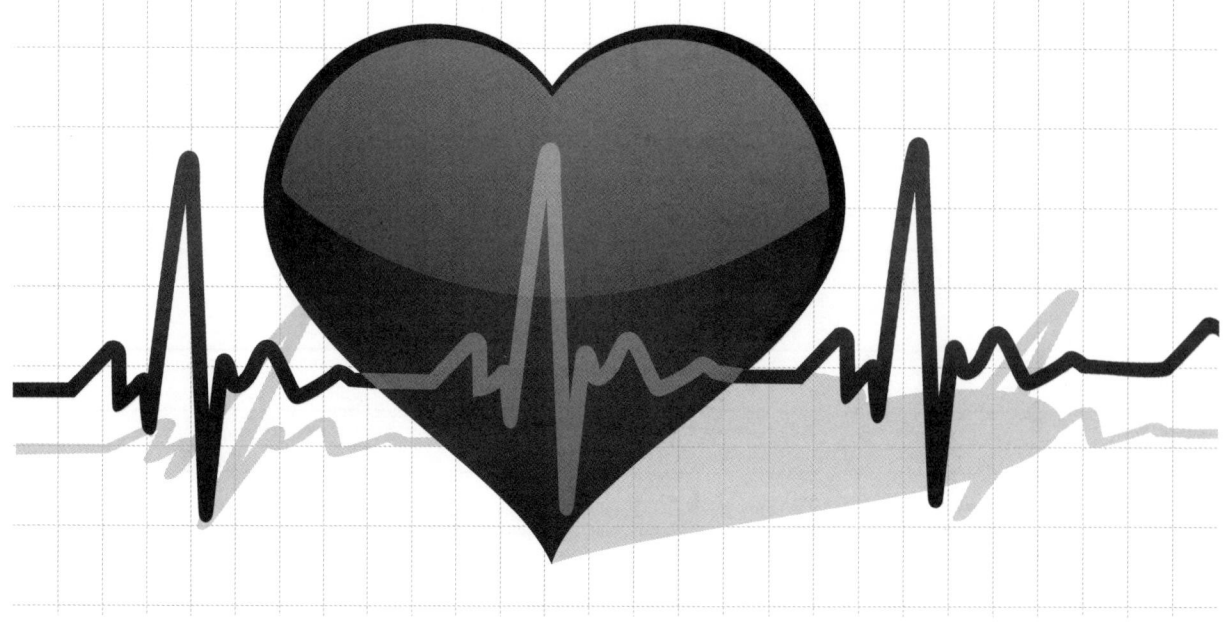

Worksheet

Expression Style Quiz

Circle one answer to complete each statement.

1. When I'm feeling angry about something, I would likely choose to:
   a. Talk with a friend
   b. Write or draw out my anger
   c. Play or listen to music
   d. Work-out or go for a run

2. When I'm feeling sad, I would be most likely to:
   a. Call someone and talk about it
   b. Write in my journal or diary
   c. Turn on some music
   d. Take a walk

3. When I'm worried about something, I find that _____ helps me.
   a. Sharing my worries with someone else
   b. Writing it down
   c. Listening to music
   d. Exercising

4. When I'm feeling happy, I really like to:
   a. Share it with others by getting together
   b. Write or create something
   c. Play or listen to my favorite song
   d. Go to the gym or for a run

5. If I'm having a rough day, I usually find that _____ helps.
   a. Talking with someone
   b. Writing out my troubles
   c. Singing along to my favorite song
   d. Making time for a good work-out

What other ways do you like to express your emotions?

_____

*Use the KEY on the back to find out more about your Emotional Expression Style.

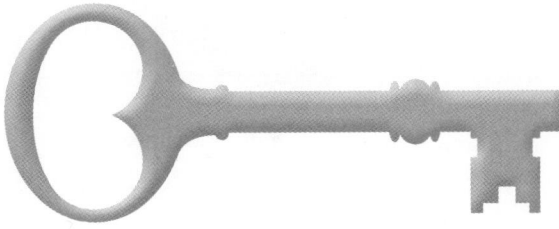

Worksheet

Expression Style Quiz KEY

Total up how many of each letter you circled on the other side and put the number beside that letter below. The letter with the highest number indicates your Expression Style. Read the description for your style below. If you don't have a number that is clearly higher than the rest, you are likely to be very diverse in the way you express your emotions.

Total	Description
a. _____	**"The Communicator"** – You are very good at communicating your feelings to others. This helps you process how you are feeling and find support.
b. _____	**"The Thinker"** – You like to put your feelings down on paper or canvas. You can gain creative energy from this process and believe feelings are important for creativity.
c. _____	**"The Musician"** – You use music as a tool for emotional expression. You understand that songs convey messages about how people feel and can use this outlet to connect with others who have felt like you are feeling.
d. _____	**"The Mover"** – You would much rather get up and get moving to express your feelings through physical movement. You can make use of the energy that comes with emotions by turning it into exercise.

Section 4: Emotional Strategies

You Can't Make Me Smile

Purpose — Individuals struggling with Self-Regulation often do not understand the power they have over their own emotions. This strategy is designed to show that they themselves have control over their own emotional responses. Others do not dictate how we feel or behave. We have the ability to control our own emotions and behaviors. Understanding this concept is critical for the development of Self-Regulation.

Materials
- You Can't Make Me Smile Worksheet

Process

1. Use the handout and the following script to introduce this activity:

    "Today we are going to play a game. We are going to try to make each other smile. We will not be able to touch each other or say anything that is inappropriate. We can tell jokes, say funny words, or make funny faces. We will take turns. First, I will try to make you smile, and then you will try to make me smile. When I try to make you smile, I want you to try not to smile and when you try to make me smile, I am going to try not to smile."

2. After a few rounds, you begin to discuss how you are able to control yourself when the other person is trying to make you smile. You might say:

    "Wow, I wonder how you were able to keep from smiling at those funny things I was doing. How did you do that?"

    Lead the individual to figure out that they were making a conscious decision to control their emotions. Maybe they were thinking of something else, or ignoring you. Use the space provided on the handout to write down the different strategies they used. This is valuable information to discuss with them and build upon to increase Self-Regulation.

3. After processing the strategies say, "What if we had changed the game to where we were trying to make each other Angry? Would we be able to use the same strategies to control our emotions?" Process this situation utilizing the strategies the individual identified.

4. End the exercise by reinforcing the fact that we control our own emotions and behaviors. Connect the lesson to real-life examples. Stress that others cannot make us feel happy, sad, scared, or angry unless we choose to. We have the power and we sure don't want to give it away to anyone!

Section 4: Emotional Strategies

You Can't Make Me Smile... (CONTINUED)

Variations

1. If working with a classroom, split into groups to create teams. One person from one team will square off against a person from another team. Repeat until everyone has had a chance to play both roles (the person trying not to smile and the person trying to make the other person smile). Keep score and whichever team has the least smiles wins. Share strategies and process together as a group.

2. If you are lacking in comedy skills, or feel uncomfortable with trying to make someone smile, you can replace that portion of the activity with watching a funny video clip, possibly from YouTube™, together while trying not to smile. With this variation, you can also count how many times the individual smiles the first time you watch the video. Then repeat the exercise with the same video at a later time and discuss how he/she was able to smile less the second time.

Worksheet

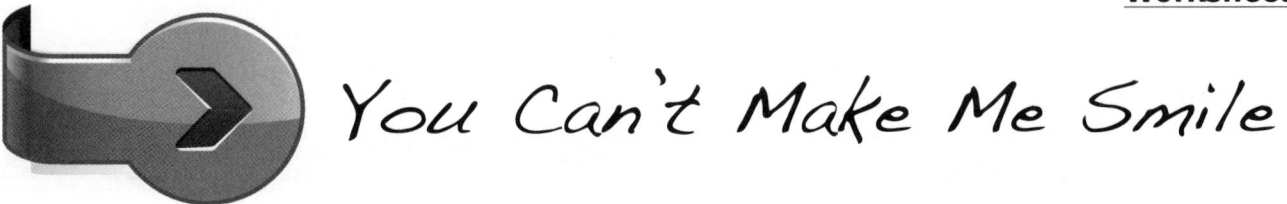
You Can't Make Me Smile

While in your seats, take turns making faces or sounds to try to get the other person to smile.

Time limit: Each person has 10 seconds to try to get the other person to smile.

Rules:
1. No touching or invading personal space during this game
2. Keep words and actions appropriate
3. Face each other and don't close your eyes
4. Have fun!

Strategies used to stay in control:

_____

_____

_____

_____

Emotional Strategies

Who's In Control?

Purpose The idea of personal control over our emotions, and responsibility for them, is central to the concept of Self-Regulation. Without understanding this concept, individuals are left feeling powerless and controlled by other people or events. This lesson is designed to help prove that we do, in fact, have the power to control our emotions, behaviors, and thoughts.

Materials
- Who's in Control Worksheet, writing utensil

Process

1. Explain that there are two types of people. Those who go through life understanding this next concept, and those who don't. The consequences of not understanding this idea are severe.

2. As you hand out the worksheet you might says something like:

    "Let's say I go to the store to buy something and they don't have what I'm looking for. I get angry about it. Did they make me angry?"

3. Discuss the answers you get to the question you posed. Then ask the students to work through the scenarios and questions on the worksheet.

Variation Draw the following on a white board: Event → Feeling. Discuss cause/effect relationships. Use examples from the Who's in Control Worksheet. Compare your first drawing to the following one as you draw it on the board: Event → _____ → Feeling. Discuss what goes in the blank.

Discussion Questions

1. What are the results of believing that other people or events control your emotions?

2. From history, what happens to groups of people who believe they have no control? How does this relate to an individual who feels that other people, or events, control their emotions?

3. Think about how often we say, or hear others say, "That made me so angry." What is implied by this statement? Can we eliminate, or think of another way to phrase, this statement?

Worksheet

Who's In Control?

1. Two girls watch the same television show together about a boy who goes on a camping trip with his father.

   Girl #1 feels happy about the show
   Girl #2 feels sad about the show

   If the show caused someone to feel a certain way, wouldn't they both have the same feeling?
   If the show doesn't cause how they feel, then what does? Explain.

   _____
   _____

2. Two groups of people go to a football game. They watch the very same game.

   Group #1 leaves feeling very happy about the game.
   Group #2 leaves feeling sad and angry about the game.

   If the game caused the people to feel a certain way, wouldn't they all feel the same?
   If the game didn't determine how they felt, then what did? Explain.

   _____
   _____

3. Jack was talking to his friend during class. His teacher asked him to stop. Jack felt angry. Who or what caused Jack to feel angry? Explain your answer.

   Could Jack change how he's feeling if he wanted to? If so, how?

   _____
   _____

4. Tommy was sitting in class. His teacher says, "It's time to line up for lunch." While Tommy was lining up, Sara bumped into him and got in front of him in the line. Tommy pushed Sara and yelled at her. The teacher sent him to the back of the line.

   Who or what caused Tommy to become so upset?
   - A. Sara
   - B. The Teacher
   - C. Tommy's own thoughts
   - D. Some other reason like he was hungry or tired

   Explain.

   _____
   _____

©YouthLight

Worksheet

Who's In Control?...(CONTINUED)

5. The other day _____

_____. I felt _____

What caused me to feel this way? How could I have changed my feelings?

_____

_____

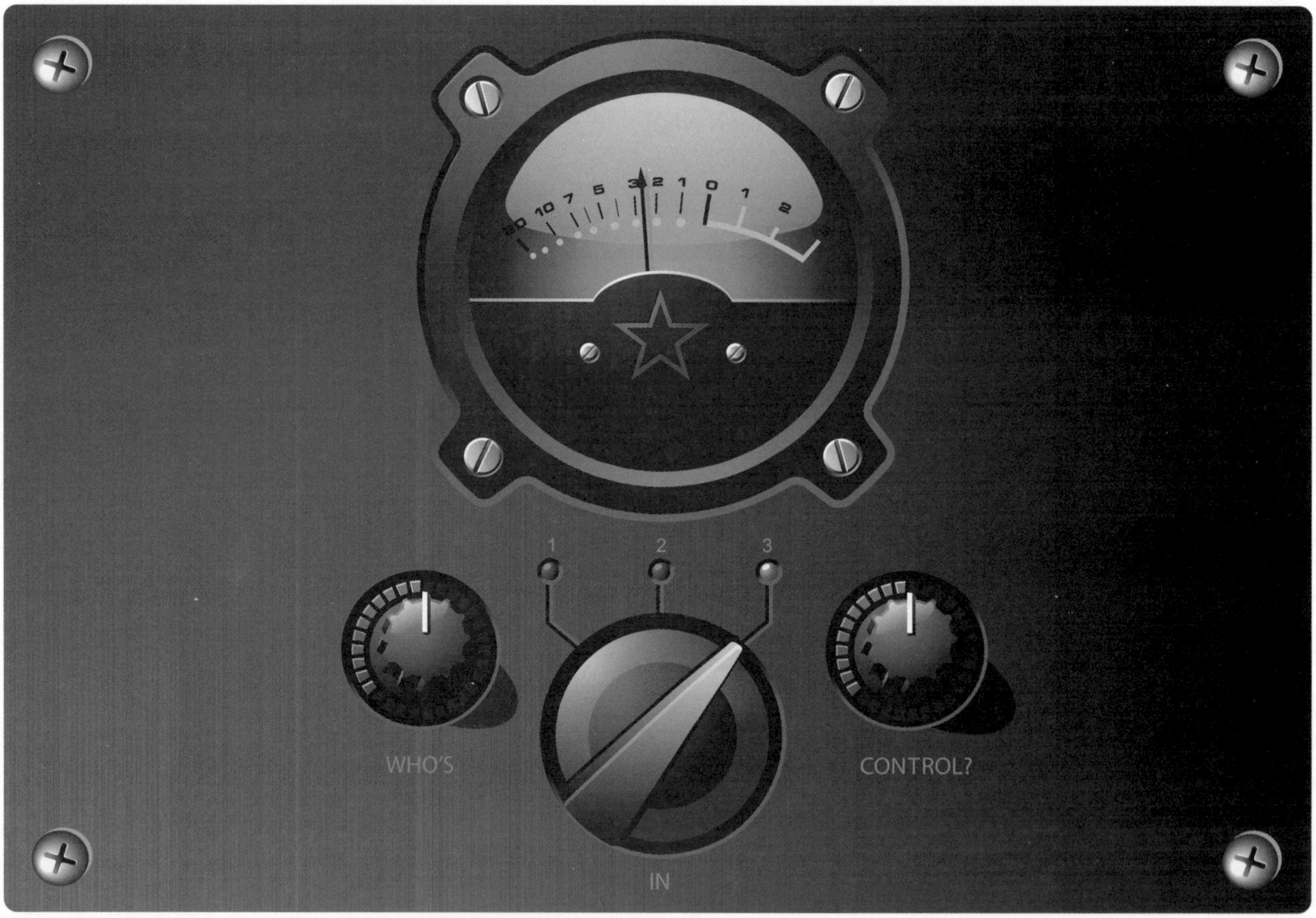

Emotional Strategies

Section 4

Declaration of Emotional Freedom

Purpose This brief activity can be combined with Who's in Control or Mind Control to emphasize that each of us has the power to control our own emotions.

Materials
- Declaration of Emotional Freedom, writing utensil

Process
1. After completing the Who's in Control or Mind Control activity, present the students with the Declaration of Emotional Freedom.

2. Read the declaration aloud as a group and fill in the blanks.

Declaration of Emotional Freedom

From this day forward, I, _____, understand that my feelings are mine and that only I can control how I feel.

Other people and events have no power over my mood unless I allow it. I know that sharing my feelings with others whom I trust is healthy for me and does not give others the power to change my feelings unless I allow it.

I will, under no circumstances, give up control of my feelings of Anger, Sadness, Fear, Happiness, etc. to anyone or anything.

This declaration I make to myself gives me the power, freedom and control to decide how I'm going to feel about anything that may happen around me. I choose what to feel, how strong I feel it and how long it lasts.

This I declare.

_____
Signature

Emotional Strategies

Mind Control

Purpose Individuals who struggle with Self-Regulation often believe that other people and events "make" them feel a certain way. They do not understand the power they have over their own feelings and behaviors. They see the relationship between an external event and their own emotional response as a cause/effect relationship. If that were true, everyone would feel and act the same way after watching the same movie. We know this is simply not true. We control our thoughts, feelings and behaviors. If one doesn't believe that he/she controls his/her own thoughts, behaviors and feelings, why would he/she try to change them? This is a critical lesson for Self-Regulation.

The following activity is designed to challenge the idea that others control our feelings and behaviors.

Materials • A remote control, Mind Control Worksheet, writing utensil

Process
1. Ask the participants if they have recently had something, or someone, that made them feel angry, scared, or sad. This is a trick question because we know that other people and events cannot make us feel a certain way. Many of the participants will likely begin to give examples because they believe that other people and things can upset them.

2. Explain that many people do not understand the power they have over their own emotions. Ask for a volunteer to help you prove a point.

3. Use your remote control to "control" the volunteer's mood. You might say:

   "Okay... I am going to use this remote control to make the volunteer feel certain ways. I am going to press the "angry button" and (volunteer's name) is going to feel angry."

4. Next, push another button and change the volunteer's mood to sad. Repeat for worried, lonely and happy.

5. The point of this demonstration is to show how silly it really is to think that others can "control" our mood. But if we believe this to be true, then we are actually giving "our remote control" over to other people and things around us. We want to be the one in charge of our feelings.

6. Ask the students to complete the Mind Control worksheet.

Section 4: Emotional Strategies

Mind Control... (CONTINUED)

Discussion Questions

1. What other evidence do we have to prove that we control our own thoughts, feelings and behaviors?

2. Why do you think that we sometimes give over control of our feelings to someone else? Maybe even someone we don't really like?

3. We often say, "That made me so upset." What does this statement imply? How can we change this phrase to be more accurate?

4. What's the relationship between the concept of controlling our own feelings and blaming others for our upset?

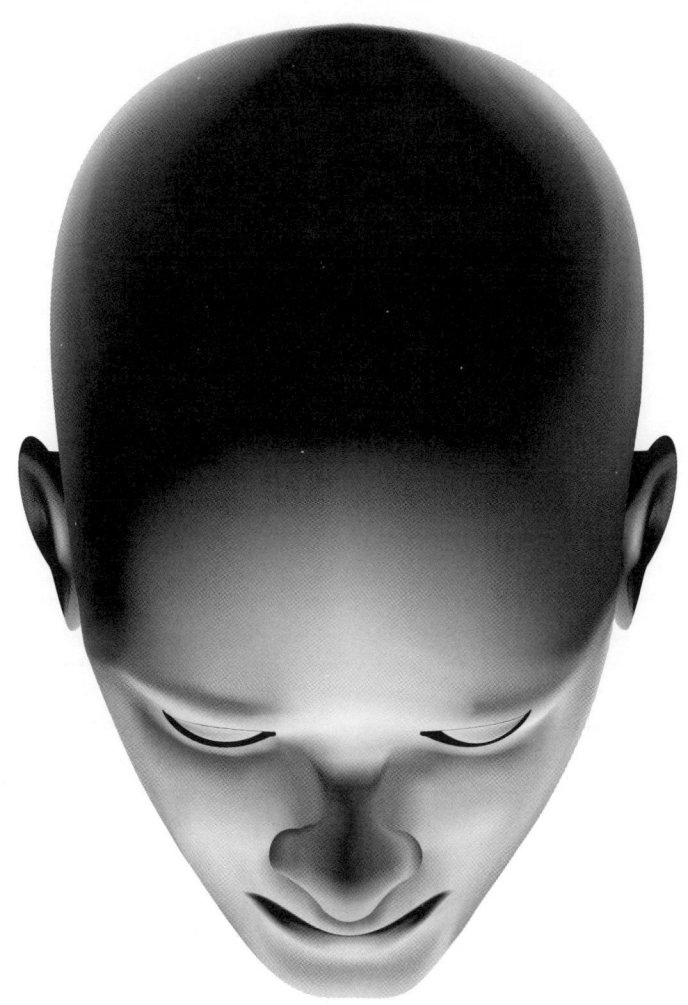

Worksheet

Mind Control

Derick

Derick and Sam do not get along. Sam often makes negative comments about the way Derick dresses, the way he plays sports, and the way he does his work. Derick feels sad and angry about the way Sam treats him. He spends time worrying about it and it clearly impacts his happiness and performance.

1. Who do you think Derick believes to be controlling his feelings? _____

2. It appears that Derick has given over his remote to someone he doesn't even like. How can Derick take back control of his remote? _____

Sophia

Sophia is going through a rough time. It just seems like things are piling up on her. She didn't make the basketball team. Her best friend moved away. Her parents are going through a divorce. She's failing History because of one bad test score. She finds herself frustrated, depressed and lonely much of the time.

1. Who do you think Sophia believes is controlling her feelings? _____

2. It appears that Sophia has given over her remote to the events happening in her life. What are some steps Sophia can take to gain control of her emotions? _____

You

Fill in the blanks with an example from your own life, similar to the two stories above.

In the past _____
_____.

I felt _____
_____.

Worksheet

Mind Control...(CONTINUED)

1. Who or what were you giving control of your emotions to?
   _____
   _____

2. This may have happened before you realized that other people/events cannot control your feelings, thoughts, or behaviors unless you allow it. What steps can you take in the future to regain control?
   _____
   _____

Section 4: Emotional Strategies

Emotional Knots

Purpose — Individuals struggling to express their emotions in healthy ways must first learn to identify and label their feelings accurately. This can be difficult, especially when the situations are complicated, or when we experience different, or even conflicting feelings about the same event. This strategy is designed to draw attention to the process of sorting out complex feelings and identifying them appropriately.

Materials
- 4 colors of yarn, shoe laces, or pipe-cleaner

Process

1. Tie the different colored pieces of yarn into a loosely knotted tangled ball.

2. Use the worksheet and the tangled ball of yarn to introduce this strategy. You might say something like:

   "Sometimes when things happen around us, we don't know how to feel about them. It can be confusing. Our feelings may get all tangled up and it's hard to sort them out, just like this tangled ball of yarn. Sometimes we need help to make sense of it all. Let's read this short story about Laura and Mary."

3. Read the short story on the worksheet together.

4. Identify a difficult event in the individual's life. Help them put the event into words in the space provided on the worksheet.

5. Help them identify the feelings he/she may have experienced during or after the event. Write the feelings in the spaces provided.

6. Present the individual with the tangled ball of yarn. Begin to process each of the feelings identified one at a time. Using the color Key, disentangle the colored yarn that corresponds to each of the emotions you process together.

Variation — Small Group – If there are issues between individuals, the entangled pieces of yarn can represent individuals within a particular situation. This can be a way to process an event that seems complicated. Assign each individual involved to a color of yarn that is in the tangled knot. As you unravel the knot one color at a time, each person will have a chance to tell their side of the story and the feelings they experienced in the situation. The goal is to promote understanding, healthy expression and ownership for feelings.

Worksheet

Emotional Knots

Short Story

Laura and Mary were best friends. Mary lived on the same street as Laura and they went to the same school. They played together almost every day for three years. Then one day, when they were in the 4th grade, Mary told Laura that she was moving away. Later that day, Laura began to cry. She decided to talk with her Mother about it. As they talked, they found out that Laura was having lots of different feelings. Here are some of the things she was feeling and why:

Sad – She thought she was losing a friend.
Angry – She thought her friend was leaving her or being taken away.
Scared – She thought she wouldn't be able to find a friend like Mary again.

Once Laura and her Mother figured out how Laura was feeling, they could talk about each one of her feelings. Once we know what our feelings are, we can figure out what to do next.

Your Story

What happened in your story?

_____

_____

_____

What feelings are in the story?

1. _____ 2. _____ 3. _____ 4. _____

Color Key:
Primary Feelings: Red = Angry   Blue = Sad   Green = Happy   Yellow = Scared/Worried
Other Feelings: Grey = Guilt/Shame   Orange = Surprise

Section 4: Emotional Strategies

Emotional Regulation Review for Mastery

Purpose As individuals move through the Self-Regulation training system, it's important to take time to review and reflect on the skills they have learned to move toward mastery. This lesson can be used as a review of the 3 Skill-training areas of Emotional Regulation:

- Identification of basic emotions
- Learn/Practice healthy ways to express emotions
- Understand/Believe that we own our emotions and are responsible for them; other people and events have no control over our emotions unless we allow it

Materials
- Emotional Regulation Review, writing utensil

Process
1. Explain that the student(s) have completed the second section of Self-Regulation Training. Refer back to the "Keys to My Success" if you are using this as a guide for your curriculum.

2. As you hand out the Emotional Regulation Review, ask them to complete the short activities to ensure that they have a good understanding of these important skills.

3. Come back together and discuss the results and complete the Optional Activities if time allows.

Worksheet

Emotional Regulation Review

Fill in the blanks.

1. Name 5 different emotions: _____, _____, _____, _____, _____

Circle the best answer.

2. Yelling and screaming are (HEALTHY or UNHEALTHY) ways to express emotions.

3. Andrew's teacher asked him to quiet down. Andrew got angry. Andrew's teacher made him angry. (TRUE or FALSE)

Complete the sentence.

4. My favorite healthy way to express my feelings is to _____
_____.

Read the scenarios and answer the questions.

Scenario #1

Dillon has a final exam in the morning. He just found out that he has to work late tonight.

What feeling(s) might Dillon be experiencing? _____

Identify two healthy ways he could express his feelings:
_____
_____

Scenario #2

Krista just overheard a conversation between a group of girls she thought were her friends. They were making very hurtful comments about her.

What feeling(s) might Krista be experiencing? _____

Identify two healthy ways she could express her feelings:
_____
_____

©YouthLight | 89

Worksheet

Emotional Regulation Review
...(CONTINUED)

Optional Activities and Discussion:

1. Share a story about the last time you felt sad, angry, worried, misunderstood, or lonely.

2. Discuss what can happen if feelings are "stuffed" for long periods of time.

3. Name as many healthy ways to express sadness as you can. Do the same for anger and worry.

4. Discuss how healthy expressive activities are similar, or different, for anger, worry, and sadness.

5. Discuss the concept of ownership and responsibility for our own feelings. This also means that we cannot control how others feel. Consider how it is true that many people do not understand this concept, and how our language also tends not to support it. For example, we often say "_____ makes me _____."

6. Discuss how a lack of ownership of our feelings can make changing behaviors difficult. Make the connection of ownership to attribution, or blame.

7. Create and perform a short skit where something challenging happens to the main character. Identify the feelings, healthy and unhealthy expressions, and signs of ownership of feelings of the characters throughout the skit.

Section 5: Cognitive Strategies

Cognitive Strategies

The strategies contained in this chapter build on the skills developed in the previous chapters and require a higher level of ability. To be ready for this level of skill, individuals should have well-developed physical calming skills, be able to identify and express emotions in healthy ways, and understand that they can exercise control over their own physical and emotional responses.

It is important to communicate that not every individual is ready for these higher level, more abstract, strategies. In particular, younger individuals and those who have significant cognitive or developmental delays may not have the ability to comprehend the concepts contained in this chapter. We have learned that having well-developed physical and emotional regulation skills will give individuals a better chance of progressing into higher level cognitive regulation and more advanced self-directed problem-solving.

The following interventions are designed to teach the basic skills of cognitive regulation. The main functional skill-training areas within the Cognitive Regulation domain are:

- Identifying and Challenging Unhealthy and Extreme Thinking
- Planning and Organizational Skills
- Problem-solving
- Gaining Insight into Motives and Healthy Ways to Get Psychological Needs Met
- Self-monitoring and Reinforcing Healthy Behaviors

Note: In addition to the Cognitive lessons in this section, Section 6 (Putting It All Together) also contains lessons that are considered to be Cognitive in nature. These lessons touch on self-monitoring, reinforcement, planning and prolem-solving.

Section 5: Cognitive Strategies

Healthy Emotional Boundaries with Technology – "WWSWW Zones"

Purpose   Many individuals who struggle with Self-Regulation have difficulty identifying and maintaining healthy social boundaries. A deficit in this area can easily be magnified in today's world with the Internet, cell phones, and social media. Sharing personal information in a public space can quickly lead to significant problems. This activity is designed to challenge individuals to think about social boundaries when expressing emotions using technology.

Materials
- WWSWW Worksheets 1 and 2, writing utensil

Process
1. Explain that we have a natural tendency to want to express our emotions to others, and that it is healthy for us to share and process our feelings with others. However, there are some things we need to think about when it comes to "who we share what with." One way we can help ourselves is to identify some boundaries in our social circles that can guide us when it comes to sharing personal information.
2. As you hand out the WWSWW (Who We Share What With) worksheet, identify all of the different ways we have of expressing our feelings to others (text, social media, notes, phone calls, blogs, etc.).
3. Ask the student(s) to complete the WWSWW worksheets 1 and 2.
4. Process the results together using the discussion questions.

Discussion Questions
1. What are the possible consequences of sharing sensitive, personal information in Zone 3?
2. Discuss how some forms of communication are more, or less, likely to go beyond the Zone you intended?
3. What controls do you have to put limits on your Zones in a digital world?
4. How does this activity relate to the concept of trust?
5. How do you determine when people move from one of your Zones to another?
6. What are the advantages to using Direct Messages to communicate personal feelings to others?
7. Discuss the permanence of communicating on the Internet.
8. Connect back to the lessons on Physical Regulation. Discuss how using your skills to calm down before you post, or message, personal information is in your best interest.

WWSWW Worksheet 1

Worksheet

Zone 1 = Immediate Family and Very Close Friends

List the people who are in your Zone 1
1. _____
2. _____
3. _____
4. _____
5. _____

Zone 2 = Extended Family, Close Neighbors and Friends

List people who are in your Zone 2
1. _____
2. _____
3. _____
4. _____
5. _____

Zone 3 = Everyone Else

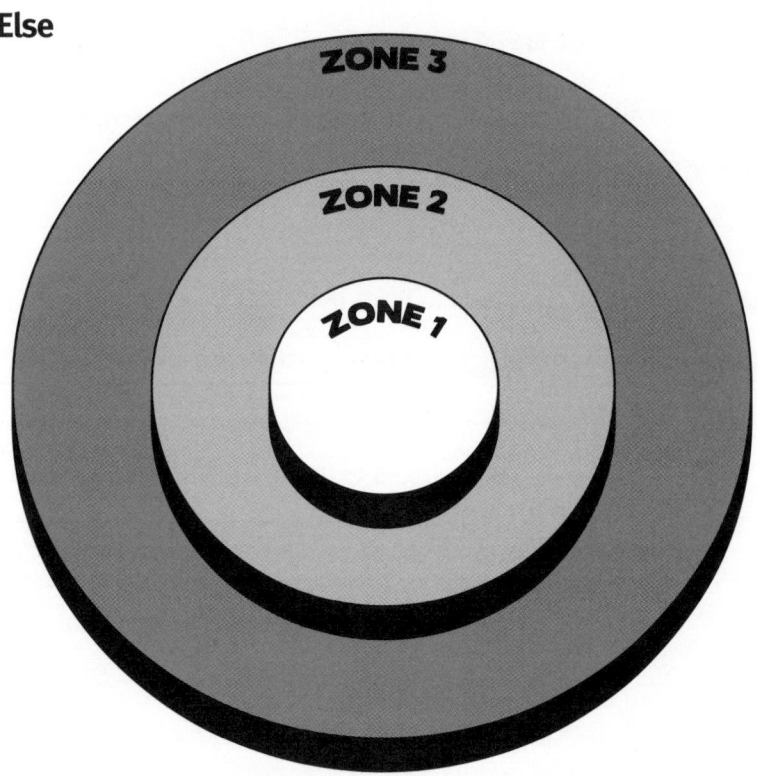

Worksheet

WWSWW Worksheet 2

Read the following situations and answer the questions.

1. You just heard that your best friend made it to nationals in gymnastics.

   What WWSWW Zone might you share this with? _____

   How might you share it (text, Internet, in person, etc.)? _____

2. You failed your Math test and are feeling sad.

   What WWSWW Zone might you share this with? _____

   How might you share it (text, Internet, in person, etc.)? _____

3. You are upset with your boyfriend/girlfriend because you heard that they like someone else.

   What WWSWW Zone might you share this with? _____

   How might you share it (text, Internet, in person, etc.)? _____

4. You have been having a lot of pain in your back lately and are going to the doctor tomorrow.

   What WWSWW Zone might you share this with? _____

   How might you share it (text, Internet, in person, etc.)? _____

5. You have a strong opinion about gun control.

   What WWSWW Zone might you share this with? _____

   How might you share it (text, Internet, in person, etc.)? _____

6. Your cat died last night.

   What WWSWW Zone might you share this with? _____

   How might you share it (text, Internet, in person, etc.)? _____

7. You are going on vacation out of state for two weeks.

   What WWSWW Zone might you share this with? _____

   How might you share it (text, Internet, in person, etc.)? _____

Section 5: Cognitive Strategies

Extreme Thinking

Purpose — Understanding that our thoughts impact our feelings/behaviors and that we can control our thoughts, therefore, control our feelings is critical for healthy Self-Regulation. This activity is designed to address and reinforce the idea that we are in control of our own emotions. It also presents the notion that unhealthy, extreme thoughts can lead to unhealthy, extreme emotions and behaviors.

Materials
- Extreme Thinking Worksheet, writing utensil

Process

1. Explain that our thoughts and beliefs are directly related to how we think and behave. You might say something like:

   → "If I go to a job interview thinking that I'm not going to get the job and I might as well not waste my time, my feelings and behaviors are going to reflect this type of thinking and also impact my appearance and performance."

2. As you hand out the worksheet, explain that many people do not understand that they can change their own mood and behavior by what they choose to think and believe. We think in words, and if our words are extreme, our feelings and behaviors will be extreme. Extreme, unhealthy thoughts usually lead to problems.

3. Ask the students to complete the worksheet.

Discussion Questions

1. What are some other common, extreme, unhealthy thoughts that can lead to problems?

2. What were some of the extreme words in the examples? Name some other extreme words to look out for.

3. If we are thinking extreme, unhealthy thoughts and feeling bad, what can we do to change our thinking? How have you accomplished this in the past?

Worksheet

Extreme Thinking

Jenny practiced all season for the state track meet. She didn't place at the meet.

She thought, "I'll never be good at this. I should just quit."

How might Jenny feel? _____

Who or what might she think caused the feeling? _____

What really caused the feeling? _____

What's a more healthy way to think about this, or what might a true friend say? _____
_____

Some of Joe's friends were all getting together and didn't invite him.

Joe thought, "They must hate me. I'm not good enough."

How might Joe feel? _____

Who or what might he think caused the feeling? _____

What really caused the feeling? _____

What's a more healthy way to think about this, or what might a true friend say? _____
_____

Lynn's teacher asked her to give a presentation to the class next week.

She thought, "Everyone will laugh at me. It will be terrible."

How might Lynn feel? _____

Who or what might she think caused the feeling? _____

What really caused the feeling? _____

What's a more healthy way to think about this, or what might a true friend say? _____
_____

Extreme Thinking ...(CONTINUED)

Taylor found out that her family is moving and she has to switch schools.

She thought, "This is awful. I hate my life."

How might Taylor feel? _____

Who or what might she think caused the feeling? _____

What really caused the feeling? _____

What's a more healthy way to think about this, or what might a true friend say? _____
_____

Russ saved up his money and bought a new phone. His little brother spilled milk all over it.

Russ thought, "I can't handle this. Everything bad happens to me."

Who or what might he think caused the feeling? _____

What really caused the feeling? _____

What's a more healthy way to think about this, or what might a true friend say? _____
_____

Lisa spent two months writing a song for the talent show. After she performed it and didn't win, she overheard one of her friends saying the song was weird.

Lisa thought, "Nobody gets me. I'm never writing again."

Who or what might she think caused the feeling? _____

What really caused the feeling? _____

What's a more healthy way to think about this, or what might a true friend say? _____
_____

Section 5: Cognitive Strategies

Calculated Risk-Taking

Purpose It's natural for those in their teenage years to want to take risks. Without this drive, we would not have the ability to leave the nest. This motivation prepares us to separate from our parents and face the world. However, those who struggle to regulate this desire can get caught-up in drugs, risky sexual behavior, and the legal system. Sometimes our natural tendency as adults is to try and extinguish this drive with restrictions and punishment. This activity is designed to ask teenagers to examine this motive and seek out healthier ways to take risks.

Materials
- Risk-Taking Quiz/Healthy Ways to Take Risks Worksheet, writing utensil

Process

1. Introduce the idea of risk-taking as a normal part of human behavior. Explain how this drive is most intense during our teenage years. You may say something like:

   → "The desire to take risks and seek out excitement is a normal part of being human. Some people have more of this desire, and some have less. However, this drive is typically the strongest when we are in our teenage years. In fact, it can be so strong during this time that teenagers can often feel invincible. Obviously, none of us are invincible and that is where this thrill-seeking drive can get us into a lot of trouble.

   Although risk-taking can have a negative impact, it also can have many positives. Without the ability to take risks, we would never want to leave home and go off to college. We would have difficulty starting relationships, driving a car, or applying for a job.

   Today we are going to take a look at this motivation of risk-taking for what it is, acknowledge that it is there, and discuss ways we can get this need met in healthy ways."

2. Ask the student(s) to complete the Risk-Taking Quiz.

3. Ask them to score their own quiz and process the results.

4. Brainstorm to generate a list of 10 healthy ways to take risks.

Discussion Questions

1. Discuss gender differences in relation to risk-taking. Did the boys score higher on the Risk-Taking Quiz? What might be some reasons?

2. How do you think your parents, or older people would score on the Risk-Taking Quiz?

Section 5: Cognitive Strategies

Calculated Risk-Taking ...(CONTINUED)

3. What are some examples of when risk-taking goes wrong?

4. What are some ways you can determine whether a risk is "healthy" or "unhealthy?"

5. Some people describe a natural high that comes from "thrill-seeking" activities. What purpose does this natural high serve? Can people become addicted to this natural high similar to drug addiction?

6. Discuss the "it won't happen to me" mentality and how it relates to the increased intensity of the risk-taking motive in adolescence.

7. Give examples of how risk-taking behaviors have been beneficial throughout our history? Consider the areas of exploration, science, art, music, and business.

Worksheet

Risk-Taking Quiz

Rate each of the following statements.

Strongly Disagree	Disagree	Maybe	Agree	Strongly Agree
1	2	3	4	5

I would like to go sky-diving. _____

I would enjoy, or do enjoy, riding a motorcycle. _____

I like movies with surprise endings. _____

When playing Truth or Dare, I would tend to choose the dare. _____

I might enjoy being dropped off in the wilderness with nothing but a knife and some duct tape. _____

I would enjoy going on a blind date. _____

Total Score _____

Healthy Ways to Take Risks
Generate a list of 10 healthy, legal ways to engage in risk-taking, or thrill-seeking.

_____
_____
_____
_____
_____
_____
_____
_____
_____

Section 5: Cognitive Strategies

Evidence Piles

Purpose From birth, each of us begins to construct belief systems about ourselves and the world around us. These beliefs become our guide for interpreting events that happen in our lives. They also play a significant role in what we pay attention to and how we decide to behave in situations. Having an awareness of this process allows us to make changes in our belief system when it becomes unhealthy. This activity is designed to provide insight into this process and create strategies for regulating our belief systems.

Materials
- White board, Evidence Piles Worksheet, writing utensil

Process

1. Explain that we create belief systems about ourselves and the world around us. You might say something like:

    "Today we are going to take a look at our beliefs about ourselves and the world. Each of us has our own set of beliefs that we use to make decisions about events that happen around us. These become our "rules for living." These beliefs also combine to make us who we are and are central to our unique personality.

    It's important to question how these beliefs are formed and what makes some beliefs stronger than others? Our beliefs are formed by evidence we gather from the world around us. One interesting thing about our beliefs is that when a belief becomes very strong, we can tend to ignore, or discount, information that goes against this belief and reach to accept information that fits with our belief.

    Whichever side has the strongest evidence is the one we will choose. This is also what happens when we change our mind about something. At some point, the evidence pile that was smaller became large enough to overtake the original belief.

    Take the example of the death penalty. Each of us has a belief about whether or not it is right or wrong. Some of us have stronger beliefs about it, and some of us have weaker positions on the topic."

2. Write the words Death Penalty on the board. Underneath it, write "In Favor" on the left side and "Opposed" on the right side.

3. Ask the students to give "evidence" to support both sides and then determine which "pile" is bigger and more convincing.

4. Indicate that this process is happening inside of us on conscious and subconscious levels.

Section 5: Cognitive Strategies

Evidence Piles ... (CONTINUED)

Process

5. As you hand out the worksheet, explain that one difficulty people can have is when a belief becomes so strong that it doesn't allow us to take in new information that could change our mind about the topic. This can cause us to become stuck and blind to any new information that could help us get "unstuck."

6. Ask the students to complete the Evidence Piles worksheet and process the experience using the Discussion Questions.

Discussion Questions

1. How can extremely strong beliefs on certain topics become dangerous if they are unhealthy?

2. How can you help others who seem "stuck" with a particular unhealthy, extreme belief?

3. Are there times when extremely positive beliefs can cause problems for people? If so, what are some examples?

4. How can these beliefs have direct impact on your mood and behavior?

Worksheet

Evidence Piles

Part 1
Shawn is 15. He grew up in the inner city. His father left when Shawn was four-years-old. Although he excels in school and sports, he seems to struggle with the idea that he is "not good enough." Even when Shawn is given a compliment, he seems to ignore it and tells himself, "Oh...they are just saying that to be nice."

Help Shawn grow his Good Enough pile.

Shawn's Piles

Part 2
There are many common beliefs that we can struggle with. Here are a few examples:

- New things are too scary to try vs. New things can be difficult, but I can overcome the fear.
- Failure is unacceptable vs. Failure is part of life. If I don't try, I won't succeed.
- I'll never be good enough vs. I am good enough. I have a lot to offer.
- Everyone is against me vs. Some people may not like me, but many do.
- Examine these examples with reference to the "piles analogy." Create piles of evidence for each side of the arguments and see if you can generate enough "evidence" for the healthy belief to be stronger than the unhealthy belief.

©YouthLight

Section 5: Cognitive Strategies

More Dirty Words

Purpose We think in words. Our thoughts directly influence the way we feel and behave. They also impact the intensity of our emotions and behaviors. The language we use to describe events around us is often a reflection of how we will feel and act in response to the event. This activity is designed to increase insight into the connections between extreme thoughts and intense emotional and behavioral responses.

Materials
- More Dirty Words Worksheet, writing utensil

Process Explain that we think in words and that the words we choose to think directly impact the way we feel and how intense our feelings and actions will be. As you hand out the More Dirty Words worksheet, explain that today's activity will help us identify some "dirty words" that lead to extremely unpleasant feelings and actions. Emphasize that our choice of words may seem trivial, but changing one word in a thought can have a profound impact on the intensity of our feelings. Ask the student(s) to complete the worksheet and process the activity together using the Discussion Questions.

Discussion Questions

1. How often do you think you use the "dirty words" you identified?

2. Look back at how you were able to rephrase the thoughts on the worksheet. Identify the emotion associated with each statement and the intensity of the emotion. Next, using your rephrased statement, re-rate the intensity of the emotion. Discuss the differences.

3. Many people throughout history have suggested that "moderation" is often the best way to happiness. How do you think this relates to the Dirty Words activity?

4. Create a plan to reward yourselves for not using these types of words for one week. Be sure to help each other by pointing out when you hear someone else using these words.

Worksheet

More Dirty Words

Rephrase these extreme thoughts into more accurate, moderate statements.

"This day is going to be horrible because I have school, work, and chores to do."
_____
_____

"I never get to do what I want."
_____
_____

"Nobody ever understands me."
_____
_____

"Everyone is going to laugh at me if I mess up."
_____
_____

"I can't stand it when this happens."
_____
_____

"This is going to take forever."
_____

List as many more "Dirty Words" as you can.
_____
_____
_____
_____

Section 5: Cognitive Strategies

Getting What You Really Want – Freedom

Purpose As human beings, we have a natural desire to make our own choices and do as we please. During adolescence this psychological need seems to intensify as we begin to create our own identity and strive for more freedom. This often results in increased conflict with authority. Challenging authority, in and of itself, is a very important skill to possess. However, there are healthy and unhealthy ways to challenge authority. This activity is designed to provide insight into this psychological drive, normalize it, and help create healthy avenues for developing this important skill.

Note: In relation to this concept, provide students with opportunities to feel like they have some freedom to make decisions about their environment. It can be helpful to allow students to make some decisions about schedules, assignments, rules, etc. when appropriate.

Materials
- Freedom Worksheet, writing utensil

Process

1. Introduce the concept of psychological needs and how it relates to freedom. You might say something like:

"As human beings we have psychological needs, just as we have physical needs like hunger and thirst. One of the needs that seem to be more intense during adolescence is the desire for freedom and the ability to make more of our own choices. As we move closer to adulthood, where we will make all of our own choices, it makes sense that this desire increases.

However, navigating this issue, and the way we choose to go about getting this need met will have significant effects on our lives as we move forward. For example, consider Jake:

He was a 16-year-old boy who had an intense desire to create his own path. He did not see the point in having rules. He would often break rules at home and at school. Then he graduated into breaking laws. This all caught up with him. Before he knew it, Jake had several people involved in his life telling him what to do. He had less freedom than when he was 14. But Jake continued to push. He now resides in an eight-by-eight cell with no freedom.

The drive for freedom is powerful, and if managed well, it can lead to great things. There are healthy and unhealthy ways to get this need met. The healthy ways will likely lead to success and happiness. The unhealthy ways will lead to failure and pain."

Cognitive Strategies

Section 5

Getting What You Really Want – Freedom
...(CONTINUED)

2. As you hand out the Freedom worksheet, you may also use the analogy of quicksand to illustrate this point. The stronger you kick and fight quicksand, the faster you sink. You need stay calm, think clearly, follow the recommended steps and implement your plan to escape quicksand.

3. Ask students to complete the Freedom worksheet and process the results using the discussion questions.

Variation Select one or more rules, or laws. Split the students into groups. Assign the groups to take opposing sides of the rule. Challenge them to debate the issues supporting and opposing the rule. Ask them to provide evidence and examples in their arguments.

Discussion Questions

1. Consider this statement. "If you want people out of your business... manage your business." What does this mean? How does it relate to the idea of personal freedom?

2. If there are rules in the classroom that you disagree with, what is the process for challenging these rules? If there isn't one, create a process.

3. Challenging a rule, even using a well thought out process, doesn't guarantee success. How does the concept of acceptance relate to this process?

4. Discuss the importance of presenting an alternative solution when challenging a current policy or rule. Also discuss the importance of gathering data and presenting evidence.

5. Consider the examples on the Freedom worksheet. How might these situations end up if the characters simply broke the rules they were dissatisfied with?

6. What are some other rules you have trouble following? What are healthy ways to address these issues?

Worksheet

Read the statements and answer the questions.

Josh has a curfew of 10:00 and would like it to be later.

How has he earned more freedom? _____

When and how might he propose this change? _____

What compromise might he be willing to propose?_____

Kayla doesn't agree with the dress code.

What do you think her issue could be? _____

How might she approach this issue? _____

What evidence could she present to support her ideas? _____

Lacey and her friends have been talking about the rules for using cell phones in their school.

What might one of their issues be?_____

How could she and her friends approach this issue in a healthy way? _____

_____

What are some options they could present? _____

Jesse thinks there is a rule at his job that actually gets in the way of good customer service.

What might this rule be? _____

What are some possible solutions? _____

How could he approach this with his boss? _____

Jessica thinks that her boyfriend's expectations about talking to other boys is too strict.

How might she approach this topic with him? _____

What might be behind her boyfriend's strict expectations? _____

_____

108 | ©YouthLight

Section 5

Cognitive Strategies

Control Debate

Purpose There is a single idea that is so central to Self-Regulation that it requires a lesson all on its own. This idea is directly related to the concepts of control, attribution and causation. The basic issue is whether one believes Diagram A to be true, or Diagram B to be true.

Diagram A: Event ----> Feeling/Behavior

Diagram B: Event ----> Thoughts ----> Feeling/Behavior

The way we believe about what "causes" our feelings/behaviors dictates how and what we will do to regulate issues with our feelings/behaviors. For example, if you believe that Events make you feel/behave in a certain way, you will look externally to try to change the Event in order to change the feeling/behavior. However, if you believe that your own Thoughts, in response to an Event, dictate how you feel/behave, then you will look internally to change the feeling/behavior. How one believes about this idea is critical for healthy self-regulation, success, and happiness. This activity is designed to clarify this theoretical divide and increase awareness of its importance.

Materials • Control Debate Worksheet, writing utensil

Process
1. Explain to the class that there are some ideas that are central to success and failure. The way we believe about certain issues can have a serious impact on our ability to be successful and happy.
2. Divide the class into two groups and explain that today's lesson involves engaging in a spirited debate of an idea.
3. Hand out the Control Debate Worksheet and ask each group to develop their arguments to be presented.
4. Read the directions on the worksheet together and proceed with the debate activity.
5. Process the Discussion Questions together. Be sure to make it clear that Diagram B supports the most healthy, self-regulated, empowered way to think about this dilemma.

Discussion Questions
1. Which team seemed to present the best case?
2. What were some of the key points that seemed to stand out in the arguments?
3. If you believe that Events cause your feelings/behaviors, how much control do you think you have over your own feelings/behaviors? How powerless are you over your own feelings/behaviors?
4. How is the idea that Events cause us to Feel/Behave in a certain way related to becoming very angry, frustrated, sad, blameful, victimized, and powerless about life?

Worksheet

Control Debate

Directions
Each team will have 5 minutes to develop their ideas that support their assigned point of view regarding the primary question about the debate scenario. Each team will have 5 minutes to present their arguments in a calm, clear, organized fashion.

Debate Scenario
Brent was having a rough day. He was up late last night studying for his math final. He learned this morning that one of his good friends is moving away. He was partnered with Sydney for his final project in history class and they were scheduled to present their project this afternoon. When Brent arrived at the history class, he found that Sydney had not completed her part of the presentation. Brent immediately began to yell and scream at Sydney. He called her names and slammed his books on the floor.

Primary Question: Who or what caused Brent to become so upset?

Team #1 - Point of View
You believe that Sydney, or the events leading up to the situation with Sydney, caused Brent to become so upset. You believe that Brent is at the mercy of his surroundings and that the events leading up to, and including Sydney's failure, caused Brent to feel and act the way he did. Diagram A illustrates your logic.

Diagram A
Event (Sydney's actions) ----> Feeling/Behavior (Anger, Yelling)

Team #2 - Point of View
You believe that, although Brent was clearly having a difficult time, his feelings and actions were a direct result of his own thoughts. You believe that Brent had the power to respond to Sydney's failure any way he chose to respond. It was his decision and it was based on how he chose to think about the event. His thoughts caused his feelings and behaviors.

Diagram B
Event ----> Thoughts ----> Feeling/Behavior

Cognitive Strategies

Section 5

Juggling Life

Purpose — Feeling overwhelmed seems to be an increasing theme for adolescents in today's world. We have all felt this way at one time or another. We know how uncomfortable it can be, but where do we learn how to move past this feeling and successfully navigate the situation? The focus of this lesson is to put the issue of feeling overwhelmed in the spotlight and provide practical, pro-active solutions for moving forward.

Materials
- Balloons, markers, Juggling Life Worksheet

Process

1. Explain that life is full of demands and challenges. We each have our list of commitments and obligations. We have school, work, activities, friends and family that require time and effort. We also have our own needs and desires to have fun and relax. How do we make time for everything in our busy lives?

2. Discuss what it's like to feel overwhelmed. Use the following example to illustrate this feeling:

   → "Riley is in honors courses, part of the dance team, the lead in the high school play, vice president of student council and on the volleyball team. She also has several friends and a large family. Riley works 10 hours every week at the local grocery store to help pay for her car. She has responsibilities at home and tries to help her grandmother around the house when she can."

3. Ask how Riley might have trouble keeping up with everything. What are all of the little things that go into having friends — birthdays, phone calls, text messages, hanging out together? What about all the little things involved in taking honors courses, or being part of the high school play, or the volleyball team?

4. Hand out the Juggling Life Worksheet and explain that there are certain skills we can develop that can help us with feeling overwhelmed.

5. Ask the students to complete the activity. Then, process the Discussion Questions together.

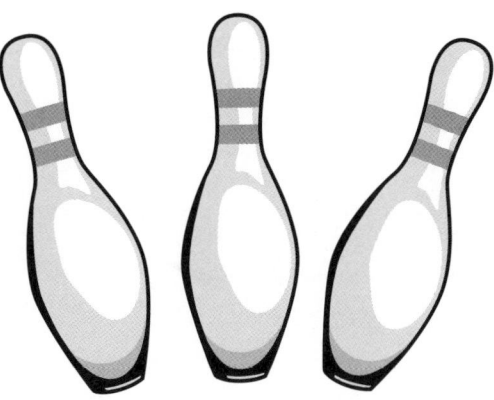

©YouthLight | 111

Section 5: Cognitive Strategies

Juggling Life ... (CONTINUED)

Discussion Questions

1. When we are overwhelmed, it often seems like we are stuck and can't move forward. What have you done in the past to help get started? Share your best Tips and Tricks from the worksheet with the rest of the group.

2. How does this analogy relate to feeling overwhelmed?

    → "Let's say your task was to climb a mountain that was there in front of you. How would you feel standing there looking at this huge mountain and thinking about everything you would need to do and all of the questions you might have about the journey? What if you were then told that you only needed to make it to a place that was a few hundred yards up the mountain by the end of the first day?"

3. How does our perception impact feeling overwhelmed?

4. Process the following examples of Tips and Tricks that can help us move forward when we feel overwhelmed.

    1. Ask for help if you need it.
    2. Make a list of what you want to accomplish and prioritize the list.
    3. Create a schedule.
    4. Remind yourself "why" you want to accomplish the items on your list.
    5. Break large tasks down into smaller, more manageable pieces.
    6. Pick out a simple task and accomplish that first. It sometimes feels good to check something off the list and it can help motivate you to continue.
    7. Watch out for Extreme Thoughts that can get in your way (Examples: I can't stand this. I'll never get it all done. I'll fail and that's unacceptable). Challenge these thoughts because they are extreme and will not help you.
    8. Remember to take care of yourself. Get enough sleep, eat healthy and build in time to exercise or relax.
    9. Many of us have different times of the day where we feel more energetic and creative. Plan your activities around these times to get the most out of your best times.

Worksheet

Juggling Life

Directions

1. Provide each student with 5 balloons to inflate.
2. Ask students to list 5 responsibilities they have in the space below. These can be long-term projects/commitments, one-time assignments, or a combination of tasks.
3. When the balloons are inflated, ask students to write each of the 5 items on one of the balloons. When they are done, they will have 5 inflated balloons, each with a different task written on it.
4. The challenge is for each student to keep all 5 balloons in the air for one minute.
5. Relate this activity to juggling our responsibilities in real life.
6. Brainstorm a list of strategies that can help with feeling overwhelmed.
7. You may want to simulate some of your ideas with the balloon analogy to see how they work. For example, one strategy may be to ask for help. See if it is easier to keep your balloons in the air with someone else helping you.

Five Responsibilities On My To Do List

1. _____
2. _____
3. _____
4. _____
5. _____

Tips and Tricks I Need to Remember When I Feel Overwhelmed:

1. _____
2. _____
3. _____
4. _____
5. _____

Section 5: Cognitive Strategies

Cognitive Regulation Review for Mastery

Purpose As individuals move through the self-regulation training system, it's important to take time to review and reflect on the skills they have learned to move toward mastery. This lesson can be used as a review for Cognitive Regulation skills:
- Identifying and Challenging Unhealthy and Extreme Thinking
- Planning and Problem-solving
- Gaining Insight into Motives and Healthy Ways to Get Psychological Needs Met
- Self-Monitoring and Reinforcement

Note: Keep in mind that there are lessons in Section 6 that also address Cognitive Regulation Skills. You may want to complete those lessons before administering the Cognitive Review.

Materials
- Cognitive Regulation Review, writing utensil

Process
1. Explain that the student(s) have completed the third section of Self-Regulation Training. Refer back to the "Keys to My Success" if you are using this as a guide for your curriculum.
2. As you hand out the Cognitive Regulation Review, ask them to complete the short activities to ensure that they have a good understanding of these important skills.
3. Come back together and discuss the results and complete the Optional Activities if time allows.

Worksheet
Cognitive Regulation Review

Fill in the blanks.

1. List 4 words that are extreme and often not helpful to use in your thinking. (*Example: Never*)

   _____, _____, _____, _____

Circle the best answer.

2. Our feelings and behaviors following an event are caused by:
   - The event
   - Our thoughts about the event

3. Kevin doesn't like one of the rules in his science class. The best way for him to address this would be to:
   a. Yell at the teacher about the rule.
   b. Break the rule whenever he feels like it.
   c. Write down his concerns about the rule and schedule a meeting with the teacher to discuss it.

Read the scenarios and answer the questions.

Scenario #1
Dillon has a final exam in the morning. He just found out that he has to work late tonight. He starts thinking, "I'll never be able to do this. I can't take it!"

If Dillon was your friend, what could you say to help him challenge those unhealthy thoughts?

_____
_____
_____
_____

Scenario #2
Krista just overheard a conversation between two girls she thought were her friends. They were making very hurtful comments about her. Krista started thinking, "Everyone hates me. I'm not good enough. I should just disappear."

If you were Krista's friend, what might you say to help her challenge these extreme, unhealthy thoughts?

_____
_____
_____
_____

# Worksheet
# Cognitive Regulation Review
...(CONTINUED)

Optional Activities and Discussion:

1. Share a recent situation where you were able to recognize your own unhealthy thoughts and effectively change them to be more healthy. Discuss how changing your thinking changed your feelings and behaviors.

2. Describe a situation where you recognized that a friend, or family member, was engaging in unhealthy, extreme thinking and you were able to help them turn it around.

3. Discuss psychological needs like the need for individual freedom and how there are healthy and unhealthy ways to get that need met. What are some other psychological needs? Discuss healthy and unhealthy ways to get those needs met. *Hint: Search basic psychological needs on the internet.*

4. Create a consequence process for catching yourself, or others, saying "_____ made me feel _____." This phrase implies that we have no control over our feelings and behaviors. The way we think about an event is what determines how we will feel and act.

5. Create and perform a short skit where something challenging happens to the main character. Identify the extreme, unhealthy thoughts the characters may have, and also how they are able to replace those thoughts with more moderate, healthy thoughts to resolve the situation. The possibilities are endless with this exercise. You may want to try a few different skits addressing different thoughts and different situations.

Section 6: Putting It All Together

After completing lessons in the physical, emotional, and cognitive areas, it's important to bring all of these concepts together. All three areas are interconnected and can impact each other. Taking the information gathered from all three areas and applying it in real life situations helps individuals add meaning to the knowledge they have acquired.

It's also important to create a plan for celebrating and reinforcing healthy regulation patterns that develop from learning these skills. Learning new skills and changing old habits can be difficult. Reinforcement and recognition are critical for long-lasting change.

Self-Regulation is a life-long process. We will not become perfect at Self-Regulation. It is as ongoing and challenging as life itself. The following activities are designed to solidify the skills students have learned throughout this process and help them recognize the changes they have made.

Section 6: Putting It All Together

Share What You Have Learned With Project-Based Learning

Purpose Now that you have covered each of the three skill-training areas of the Self-Regulation Training System, it's time to synthesize and solidify the information. Project-based learning is an excellent way for individuals to increase and share the skills they've acquired. This activity is designed to provide an avenue for individuals to showcase, reinforce and share their new Self-Regulation skills.

Note: This lesson will need to be spread out over two or three sessions.

Materials
- Self-Regulation Project Worksheet, writing utensil, supplies identified for projects

Process

1. Explain to the group that they have learned several skills they can use to live longer, be happier, and have more success. Now it's time to put those ideas together into a project that will be used to help others learn about Self-Regulation.

2. Divide into groups and hand-out the Self-Regulation Project Worksheet.

3. In this first session the groups will brainstorm to determine which project they will complete, provide a brief summary, indicate group member roles, and develop a supply list.

4. Between sessions, supplies will be gathered and brought to the next session.

5. Session two is used for creating the project.

6. In session three the groups will present their projects to the larger group.

Discussion Questions

1. Is this a project that you can share with others over the Internet?

2. Working as a team can often provide us with great opportunities to use our Self-Regulation skills. Did any situations arise when creating your project that allowed you to use the skills you've learned?

Worksheet

Self-Regulation Project

Now that you've become an expert on Self-Regulation skills, we need to be the teacher. Select a project type below and create something that can be used to teach others about the skills you've learned to have a long, happy, successful life; be creative, think outside the box, consider using technology to help spread the word and share your completed project with others.

Project Options:

Create a video to teach the concepts you have learned. You may want to act out a skit of an everyday situation and point out how using Self-Regulation skills can impact the outcome.

Create a poster that represents one, or more, of the Self-Regulation skills that could be hung in the school to help educate and remind your peers how to regulate themselves.

Create a new activity that could be used to teach one of the Physical, Emotional, or Cognitive skills for Self-Regulation.

Write a song or poem that contains concepts from the Self-Regulation Training System.

Have an idea that's not listed here, but would be great? Ask the adult in charge to see if it will work, and if so, go for it!

Provide a Brief Summary of Your Plan:

_____

_____

_____

Who's doing what? Assign duties and roles for the group members.

_____

_____

_____

What supplies will you need? Create a supply list and check it out with the adult in charge.

_____

_____

_____

Section 6: Putting It All Together

Plan of Action

Purpose Most of us have at least one area of our life that we struggle to regulate. It may be an unhealthy habit we have, something from our past, or a relationship that's troublesome. We may have tried to change it before with little success. But if you've progressed, practiced and mastered the Physical, Emotional and Cognitive skills of Self-Regulation, you now have some extremely powerful tools to create a successful plan of attack. This strategy is designed to help individuals apply the skills they've learned from the Self-Regulation Training System to a particular problem area and create a Plan of Action.

Materials
- Plan of Action Worksheets, writing utensil

Process
1. Explain that we each have our own areas to work on and that this process is ongoing throughout our lives. You might say something like:

    "We all have our own strengths and challenges. As we go through our lives, there will be certain areas that need work. We develop habits and experience struggles that can impact our mood and behaviors in negative ways. But throughout the Self-Regulation training, we've gained powerful tools for regulating these issues.

    Today we are going to take a look at one area of our life that we would like to make some changes. We are going to apply the tools we learned to a particular issue that will help us become happier and more successful."

2. As you hand out the Plan of Action worksheets, indicate that the first worksheet is a sample of how Aaron put together a simple plan using the Self-Regulation skills to fix a problem he was having.

3. Explain that the second worksheet is for each individual to identify a problem area and create a solution based on the Self-Regulation skills they've learned.

4. Encourage them to use their Keys to My Success list in the process.

5. Process the activity using the discussion questions.

Variation Get with a partner, or get a small group together, and help each other brainstorm ideas for addressing the issues each member of the group wants to target with their Plan of Action.

Discussion Questions
1. What barriers can get in the way of making the change you identified? Consider the "rewards" you experience for staying the same and not changing the behavior.
2. Discuss your level of commitment to making this change. Rate it on a scale of 1-100 and process your rating.
3. Discuss the difficulties you've seen with others who have tried to make changes in their own behavior. What could they have done that may have increased their chances of success?
4. In what other areas might you use your newly acquired Self-Regulation skills in the future?

Worksheet

Plan of Action (Sample)

What's the Problem?
Aaron notices that his test scores are slipping. After learning about Self-Regulation, he realizes that he worries about his tests. He studies, but when it's test time, it seems like his mind goes blank. He notices that his heart races and he has trouble sleeping the night before a big test. He is frustrated because he does well on the daily work, but his overall grade is low because of the tests.

What's the Plan?

Physical Regulation
What are the physical regulation pieces you can address?
1. My warning system is activated when I know the test is coming.
2. My heart beats fast, I feel sweaty, and my mind goes blank.
3. I have trouble sleeping the night before the test.

How will you address these issues?
1. I will recognize my warning signs when I feel them.
2. When I notice warning signs, I will go to my safe place or use one of my calming skills to shut down the warning system.
3. I will stick to my routine the night before a test and use my calming skills before I go to bed.

Emotional Regulation
What are the emotional regulation pieces you can address?
1. I feel worried about failing the test.
2. Now I also feel more worried that I will "go blank" again.
3. I am frustrated because I spend time studying and know the information_

How will you address these issues?
1. I have identified that I am feeling worried and frustrated.
2. I will listen to music, go for a walk, or play my guitar, or talk with someone to express these feelings.
3. I understand that my feelings are mine and the test does not "make me worry"- So that means I can fix this.

Cognitive Regulation
What are the cognitive regulation pieces you can address?
1. I'm having extreme thoughts about the test like; "I can't stand it if I fail, I'm going to do terrible on the test, everyone will think I'm stupid if I do badly."
2. My study habits could be better, the classes have gotten more difficult and I may have to put more time in to studying than I did before.

How will you address these issues?
1. I will recognize the extreme, unhealthy thoughts when they come and I will challenge them with more accurate statements like, "I will do the best I can and that's good enough; I can stand it if I get a low grade. It's not the end of the world."
2. I will set up a better study schedule and manage my time more effectively leading up to the test. I can use my calendar to set study times.

What are your rewards for making these changes?
1. Better grades
2. Not feeling frustrated and worried about tests

Plan of Action

Worksheet

What's the Problem?

_____
_____
_____

What's the Plan?

_____
_____
_____
_____

Physical Regulation

What are the physical regulation pieces you can address?

1. _____
2. _____
3. _____

How will you address these issues?

1. _____
2. _____
3. _____

Emotional Regulation

What are the emotional regulation pieces you can address?

1. _____
2. _____
3. _____

How will you address these issues?

1. _____
2. _____
3. _____

Worksheet

Plan of Action ...(CONTINUED)

Cognitive Regulation

What are the cognitive regulation pieces you can address?

1. _____
2. _____
3. _____

How will you address these issues?

1. _____
2. _____
3. _____

What other strengths do you have that can help you make this change?

_____
_____
_____

What supports do you need to make this change?

_____
_____
_____

What are your rewards for making these changes?

_____
_____
_____

Section 6: Putting It All Together

Celebrate Success

Purpose As you have probably noticed, the Self-Regulation Training System is largely focused on skill development, rather than rewards and punishment. However, self-monitoring and responsibility are key underlying themes. Once a skill has been taught and practiced, we want to celebrate healthy skill development and reinforce new behaviors.

This activity is designed to create a plan for celebrating the use of the Self-Regulation skills that have been learned.

Materials
- Celebrate Success Worksheet, writing utensil

Process
1. Explain that Self-Regulation is a life-long process. We will never be perfect at regulating our feelings and behaviors. However, we can get better at it.

2. As you hand out the Celebrate Success Worksheet, explain that it is important to recognize where we started and where we are now. It's also important to acknowledge our successes and reward ourselves.

3. Ask the students to brainstorm about possible rewards that are simple and affordable. Then ask them to complete the items in Part 2, similar to the examples provided on the worksheet. They may want to use the Keys to Success form to help them complete this activity.

Discussion Questions
1. In this activity we have identified ways you can reward yourself, but what are the other rewards that come from changing the behaviors you've identified?

2. What are some ways you can help others around you by reinforcing the changes they've made?

3. As a group, what are some ways to acknowledge when someone uses a Self-Regulation skill? Set some goals and create a reinforcement system for the group.

Worksheet

Celebrate Success

Part 1 - Brainstorm list of possible rewards:

_____

_____

_____

_____

Part 2 – Fill in the Blanks Below

Examples:

When I communicate my worries in a healthy way, I will treat myself by buying that new song I've been wanting to download.

When I go one month without having a blow-up, I will treat myself to dinner at that new restaurant downtown.

Behavior #1

When I _____

I will _____

_____

Behavior #2

When I _____

I will _____

_____

Behavior #3

When I _____

I will _____

_____

Section 7: Core Curriculum Guide

The goal of the Self-Regulation Training System is for individuals to learn the skills necessary for healthy physical, emotional and cognitive regulation in order to be happy and successful. A great deal of success has been achieved by delivering Self-Regulation Training in a series of 12 Sessions over a 6-week period of time to individuals, small groups and classrooms around the country. Each session is approximately 20 minutes long.

The following is a sample of how to put together and deliver a 12-session Core Curriculum. You will notice that this example does not move particularly far into the Cognitive Regulation Domain. Please feel free to use additional self-regulation lessons to supplement the curriculum, or as booster sessions.

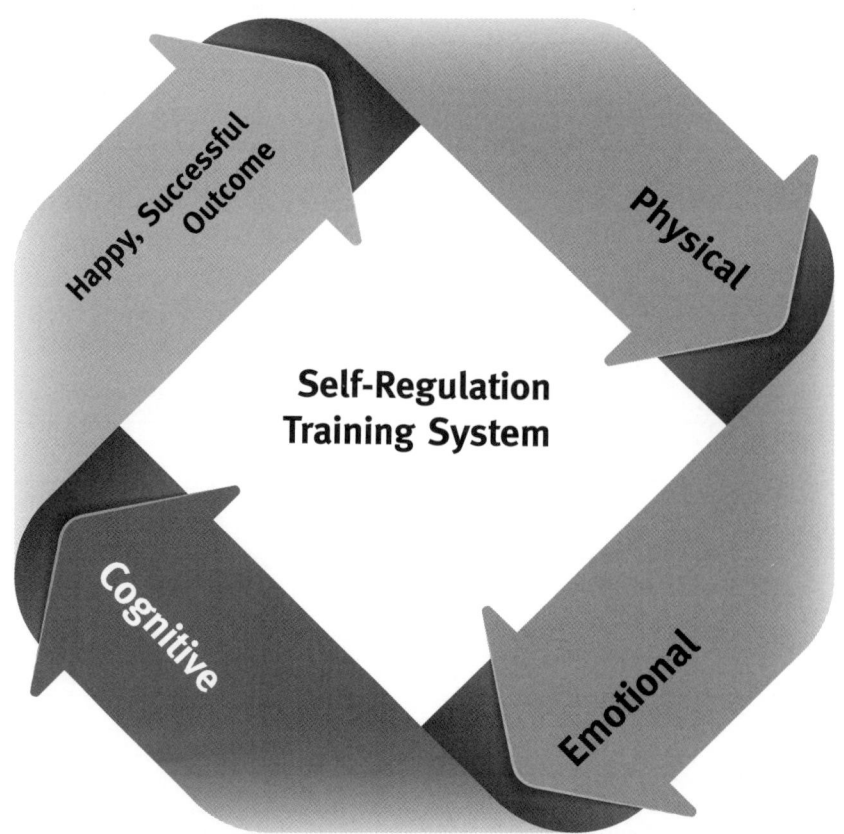

Section 7: 12-Session Core Curriculum for Self-Regulation Training

Before Session 1
- Send home the Parent Letter (see Appendix)
- Collect baseline data – Teacher Rating Scale (See Appendix)
- Folder for each student to keep their Self-Regulation materials in
- If collecting data, be prepared to track attendance for each session

Session 1

Focus of this session:
- Link success to self-regulation skills

Activities and Lessons:
- If collecting data, administer Student Self-Report Questionnaire (See Appendix)
- Distribute student folders
- Complete the lesson titled Keys to My Success (p.18)
- Complete the lesson titled Regulate for Success (p.24)

Session 2

Focus of this session:
- Recognize physical warning signs of upset

Activities and Lessons:
- Complete the lesson titled My Warning Signs along with Variation #1 (p.35)

Note: It's best to do the student presentation first.

Session 3

Focus of this session:
- Examine emotional threats and ways to shut down the warning system

Activities and Lessons:
- Complete the lesson titled Alarms and False Alarms (p.30)
- Complete the lesson titled Stretching and Movement (p.43)

Session 4

Focus of this session:
- Create a sense of safety to shut down the warning system

Activities and Lessons:
- Complete the lesson titled Create a Safe Place (p.38)
- Complete the lesson titled Mobile Safety (p.41)

12-Session Core Curriculum for Self-Regulation Training

Session 5 Focus of this session:
- Accurately identify emotions

Activities and Lessons:
- Complete the lesson titled What's Your Status? (p.56)
- Complete the lesson titled Feelings Play List (p.58)
- Update Keys to My Success worksheet from Session #1

Session 6 Focus of this session:
- Identify healthy ways to express emotions

Activities and Lessons:
- Complete the lesson titled Emotional Build-up (p.62)
- Complete the lesson titled Healthy Expression Skits (p.70)

Session 7 Focus of this session:
- Strengthen understanding of healthy emotional expression

Activities and Lessons:
- Complete the lesson titled Advice Blog (p.65)
- Complete the lesson titled Expression Style Quiz (p.72)
- Complete the lesson titled Top 10 List (p.68)

Session 8 Focus of this session:
- Understanding that we control our own feelings and behaviors

Activities and Lessons:
- Complete the lesson titled You Can't Make Me Smile with Variation #1 (p.75)

Session 9 Focus of this session:
- Reinforce the idea that we control our own thoughts, behaviors, and feelings

Activities and Lessons:
- Complete the lesson titled Who's in Control (p.78)
- Complete the lesson titled Declaration of Emotional Freedom (p.81)
- Update Keys to My Success worksheet from Session #1

12-Session Core Curriculum for Self-Regulation Training

Session 10 **Focus of this session:**
- Gain understanding of healthy versus unhealthy thoughts

Activities and Lessons:
- Complete the lesson titled Extreme Thinking (p.95)
- Complete steps 1, 2, and 3 from the lesson titled Share What You've Learned with Project-based Learning (p.118) – Remember to bring identified project supplies to Session #11.

Session 11 **Focus of this session:**
- Strengthen and synthesize self-regulation skills through project-based learning

Activities and Lessons:
- Continue to work on group projects from lesson titled Share What You've Learned with Project-based Learning(p.118)

Session 12 **Focus of this session:**
- Strengthen and synthesize self-regulation skills through project-based learning

Activities and Lessons:
- Finish lesson titled Share What You've Learned with Project-based Learning (p.118) with the project presentations.
- If collecting data, administer Student Self-Report Questionnaire (See Appendix)
- Complete Keys to My Success Worksheet from Session #1 with skills learned

After Session 12
- If collecting data, complete Teacher Rating Scale again (See Appendix)
- Create a plan to integrate materials into every-day interactions
- Explore opportunities for delivering booster sessions to maintain self-regulation skills
- Create a plan to reinforce the use of self-regulation skills (i.e. – reward system)

Appendix A

Individual Student – Assessment/Progress Monitoring Tool

Rate each on a scale of 1 to 10 with 10 being well-developed.

	Behaviors To Address/Goals	1st Rating (1-10)	Strategy Used (See Matrix)	Response	Outcome Rating (1-10)
PHYSICAL					
Recognizes physical signs					
Uses healthy calming strategies successfully					
EMOTIONAL					
Identifies feelings					
Recognizes responsibility and ability to change					
Expresses emotions in healthy ways					
COGNITIVE					
Replaces unhealthy thoughts with healthy beliefs					
Uses cognitive strategies to problem-solve					
STRENGTHS:			**BARRIERS:**		

Appendix B

Diagram of Self-Regulation Training Philosophy

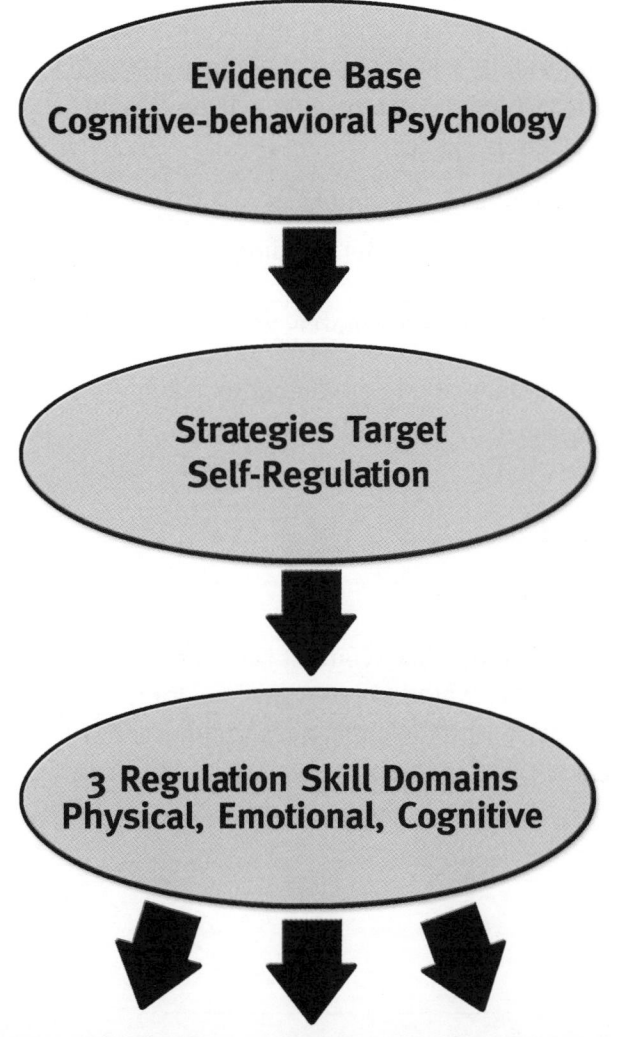

Academic Performance	Emotional Control	Motivation
Aggression/Violence	Executive Function	School Safety
Anger	Impulse Control	Self-efficacy
Anxiety	Learned Helplessness	Self-esteem
Attention	Locus of Control	Social interaction
Attribution	Longevity	Success
Cognitive Flexibility	Happiness	Trauma
Depression	Oppositional Defiance	Well-being

Appendix C

Parent Letter

Dear Parent or Guardian:

This letter is to inform you of the opportunity your teen has been given to participate in an interactive Self-regulation Training Program. This program utilizes interactive, engaging activities to increase your teen's ability to:
- Physically calm down when he/she is upset
- Identify and express his/her emotions appropriately
- Implement problem-solving skills and gain understanding

The program consists of 8-12 brief sessions (approximately 20 minutes each).

Research indicates that those with well-developed Self-Regulation skills:
- Have better academic performance
- Do better socially
- Have fewer mental health issues
- Live longer, happier lives

As with all things involving education, parental involvement is the key to success. Your teen may be asked to speak with you about what he/she is learning. We would like to thank you for taking part in this important step toward preparing your teen with the tools to cope with the challenges that he/she will face in life.

Sincerely,

_____

Appendix D

Self-Regulation Training Contract for Change

I _____, want to be successful. Over the next few weeks I will try my best to help myself by learning these important skills. When I complete my training I will be able to calm myself down, express my feelings in healthy ways, and create solutions for some of the things I've been struggling with. Use the next few lines to briefly describe a situation that has been troubling you. It could be something that you would like to learn how to solve on your own.

_____
_____

***Complete the lower portion after you have completed your training.**

Situation for Self-regulator to Process:

1. What happened? _____
   _____
   _____

2. How did your body feel? _____
   _____
   _____

3. What were your feelings? And how much?

   Feelings: _____
   _____

   How much (1-10)? _____

4. What were your thoughts about what happened? _____
   _____
   _____

Appendix D ...(CONTINUED)

Self-Regulation Strategies:

1. Physical – What did you do to calm your body down? How did you do?

   _____
   _____
   _____

2. Emotions – What did you do to express your feelings? Was it healthy?

   _____
   _____
   _____

3. Cognitive – Were your thoughts about the event accurate and healthy? What's the plan if this happens again?

   _____
   _____
   _____

Appendix E

Event Processing Worksheet

Information:

1. What happened? _____
   _____

2. Any Warning Signs? _____
   _____

3. What did you feel? And how much? _____

   Feelings: _____
   _____

   How much (1-10)? _____
   _____

4. What were your thoughts about what happened? _____
   _____
   _____

Self-Regulation Strategies:

1. Physical – What did you do to calm your body down? How did you do? ___
   _____
   _____

2. Emotions – What did you do to express your feelings? Was it healthy? ___
   _____
   _____

3. Cognitive – Were your thoughts about the event accurate and healthy? What's the plan if this happens again? _____
   _____
   _____

Appendix F

Self-Regulation Student Questionnaire

First Name: _____ Last Name: _____

Birth date: _____ Gender (M/F): _____ Today's Date _____

Directions: Read the statements and then circle the answers that best describe you.

Do Not Mark

1. When I get upset, I calm down pretty quickly.
   Almost Never | Not very Often | Sometimes | Most of the Time | Almost Always

2. I am able to calm myself down when I need to.
   Almost Never | Not very Often | Sometimes | Most of the Time | Almost Always

3. I hit, yell or throw things when I get upset.
   Almost Never | Not very Often | Sometimes | Most of the Time | Almost Always

4. I try to relax when I feel that I am starting to get upset.
   Almost Never | Not very Often | Sometimes | Most of the Time | Almost Always

5. I tell others how I'm feeling.
   Almost Never | Not very Often | Sometimes | Most of the Time | Almost Always

6. I keep my feelings locked up inside.
   Almost Never | Not very Often | Sometimes | Most of the Time | Almost Always

7. My feelings get out of control.
   Almost Never | Not very Often | Sometimes | Most of the Time | Almost Always

8. When I have bad thoughts, I can get them out of my head.
   Almost Never | Not very Often | Sometimes | Most of the Time | Almost Always

9. When something is going wrong, I make a plan to solve it.
   Almost Never | Not very Often | Sometimes | Most of the Time | Almost Always

10. I change my thoughts to be more positive when I'm upset.
    Almost Never | Not very Often | Sometimes | Most of the Time | Almost Always

Appendix F ...(CONTINUED)

11. Name 4 feelings:

    1. _____
    2. _____
    3. _____
    4. _____

12. Please read this short story and answer the question.

    Tommy was sitting in class. His teacher said, "It's time to line up for lunch." While Tommy was lining up, Sara bumped into him and got in front of him in the line. Tommy pushed Sara and yelled at her. The teacher sent him to the back of the line.

    Who or what caused Tommy to become so upset? Choose the best answer.

    A. Sara
    B. The teacher
    C. Tommy's own thoughts
    D. Some other reason like he was hungry or tired

Do Not Mark

Scoring Instructions for Self-Regulation Student Self-Report Questionnaire

Questions 1-10 are each worth 5 points and scored on a scale of 1-5 with "Almost Never" receiving a score of 1 and "Almost Always" receiving a score of 5. Questions 3, 6 and 7 are reverse-scored.

Question 11 requires some judgment about which responses to accept. Do not accept physical feelings such as tired or hungry. We are looking for emotions like happy, sad, excited, lonely, disappointed, loss, mad, angry, hopeless, hopeful, embarrassed, frustrated, jealous, surprised, content, scared, worried, nervous, etc.

0 or 1 correct responses receives 1 point.
2 or 3 correct responses receives 3 points.
4 correct responses receives all 5 points.

Question 12 is scored 0 or 5 points. C is the best answer and receives a score of 5 points. All other answers receive a score of 0.

Appendix G

Self-Regulation Teacher Rating Scale

Directions: Please provide each student's name, birth date and gender and your own details. Then, rate each student on a scale of 1-10 in the following areas. For each item, think about all opportunities the student had to demonstrate the concept or behave in the way described. You may use any number from 1-10. For instance:

- Rate the student "1" if he/she never behaved that way
- Rate the student "5" if he/she behaved that way about half the time
- Rate the student "10" if he/she almost always behaved that way

Please give your best estimate; do not leave any blanks.

Student Name	Date of Birth (Use MM/DD/YY format)	Enter Gender (M = Male, F = Female)	Demonstrates knowing his/her warning signs of becoming upset.	Uses calming strategies to prevent getting upset.	Demonstrates knowing healthy ways to express anger, sadness and worry.	Interacts well with peers.	Seeks attention and social contact in healthy ways.	Follows classroom rules and directions.	Demonstrates knowing a healthy calming strategy.	Uses words to label and communicate basic feelings to others.	Demonstrates understanding that others can't "make" him/her feel upset.	Demonstrates knowing skills to cope with change.	Is focused and alert at an age-appropriate level.	Is capable of improving his/her ability to self-regulate this school year.
e.g., Justin Applewood	11/11/00	M	3	3	2	3	3	2	3	2	2	2	1	5

Appendix H

Self-Regulation = Success
3 Steps

- Physical Strategies →
- ↑ Emotional Strategies
- ← Cognitive Strategies

References

Bailey, B. A., (2001). *Conscious discipline: 7 basic skills for brain smart classroom management.* Oviedo, Fl: Loving Guidance, Inc.

Baumeister, R. F., Heatherton, T. F., & Tice, D. M. (1994). *Losing control: How and why people fail at self-regulation.* San Diego: Academic Press.

Beck, R., & Fernandez, E. (1998). Cognitive-behavioral therapy in the treatment of anger: A meta-analysis. *Cognitive Therapy and Research, 22*(1), 63-74.

Butler, A. C., Chapman, J. E., Forman, E. M., & Beck, A. T. (2006). The empirical status of cognitive-behavioral therapy: A review of meta-analysis. *Clinical Psychology Review, 26,* 17-31.

Cannon, W. B. (1932). *The Wisdom of the Body.* New York: W.W. Norton.

Chapin, B. & Penner, M. (2012). *Helping young people learn self-regulation.* Chapin, SC: Youthlight Publishing.

Duckworth, A. L. & Seligman, M. E. (2005). Self-discipline outdoes IQ in predicting academic performance in adolescents. *Psychological Science, 16*(12), 939-944.

Ellis, A. (1962). *Reason and emotion in psychotherapy.* Secaucus, NJ: Citadel Press, Pages 24-32.

Goleman, D. (1998). *Working with emotional intelligence.* New York: Bantam Books.

Greene, R. W., & Ablon, J. S. (2006). *Treating explosive kids: The collaborative problem solving approach.* New York: The Gilford Press.

Grossarth-Maticek, R. & Eysenck, H. J. (1995). Self-regulation and mortality from cancer, coronary heart disease, and other causes: A prospective study. *Personality and Individual Differences, 19*(6), 781-795.

Hubble, M.A., Duncan, B.L., & Miller, S.D. (eds.) (1999). *The heart and soul of change: What works in therapy.* Washington, D.C.: APA Press.

Kuhl, J. (1984). Volitional aspects of achievement motivation and learned helplessness: Toward a comprehensive theory of action control. In B. A. Maher (Ed.), *Progress in experimental personality research* (Vol. 13, pp. 99-171). New York, NY: Academic Press.

Macklem, G. L. (2008). *Practitioner's guide to emotion regulation in school-aged children.* New York, NY: Springer.

Masten, A. S., & Coatsworth, J. D. (1998). The development of competence in favorable and unfavorable environments: Lessons from research on successful children. *American Psychologist, 53,* 205-220.

Moffitt, T. E., Arseneault, L., Belsky, D., Dickson, N., Hancox, R. J., Harrington, H., Poulton, R., Roberts, B. W., Ross, S., Sears, M. R., Thomson, W. M., & Caspi, A. (2011, February). A gradient of childhood self-control predicts health, wealth, and public safety. *Proceedings of the National Academy of Sciences, 108*(7), 2693-2698.

Perry, B. D. (2006). The neurosequential model of therapeutics: Applying principles of neurodevelopment to clinical work with maltreated and traumatized children. In N. B. Webb (Ed.), *Working with traumatized youth in child welfare* (pp. 27-52). New York, NY: The Guilford Press.

Shonkoff, J. P., Phillips, D., & National Research Council (U.S.). (2000). *From neurons to neighborhoods: The science of early child development.* Washington, D.C: National Academy Press.

Yerkes, R.M. & Dodson, J.D. (1908). The relation of strength of stimulus to rapidity of habit-formation. *Journal of Comparative Neurology and Psychology,* 18, 459-482.

About the Author

Brad Chapin, M.S. is a husband and a father of three. He is a Masters Level Psychologist and Licensed Clinical Psychotherapist. He is an author, international speaker, and expert in the area of Self-Regulation Training. He is also the creator of many tools used for helping children and teenagers learn the skills necessary for healthy self-regulation, including the Challenge Software Program for children and the Self-Regulation Training Board.

Brad has been working with individuals and families for over 10 years. He spends a great deal of time training school counselors, teachers, mental health professionals and parents how to implement self-regulation strategies successfully. He also serves as the Director for Community-based Services for his local Community Mental Health Center where he oversees children's mental health services delivered by 75 staff members in the homes, schools, and communities throughout a five-county area.

Website: www.selfregulationtraining.com

Email: brad.chapin@cpschallenge.com